Healthy Relationships

Recent Titles in
Q&A Health Guides

HEALTHY
RELATIONSHIPS

Your Questions Answered

Charles A. McKay

Q&A Health Guides

An Imprint of ABC-CLIO, LLC
Santa Barbara, California • Denver, Colorado

Copyright © 2023 by ABC-CLIO, LLC.

Library of Congress Cataloging-in-Publication Data

Names: McKay, Charles A., author.
Title: Healthy relationships : your questions answered / Charles A. McKay.
Description: Santa Barbara, California : Greenwood, [2022] | Series: Q&A
  health guides | Includes bibliographical references and index.
Identifiers: LCCN 2022041765 | ISBN 9781440878916 (hardcover) | ISBN
  9781440878923 (ebook)
Subjects: LCSH: Teenagers—Sexual behavior. | Interpersonal attraction. |
  Interpersonal relations. | Interpersonal conflict.
Classification: LCC HQ27 .M3925 2022 | DDC 306.70835—dc23/eng/20220914
LC record available at https://lccn.loc.gov/2022041765

ISBN: 978-1-4408-7891-6 (print)
      978-1-4408-7892-3 (ebook)

27 26 25 24 23   1 2 3 4 5

This book is also available as an eBook.

Greenwood
An Imprint of ABC-CLIO, LLC

ABC-CLIO, LLC
147 Castilian Drive
Santa Barbara, California 93117
www.abc-clio.com

This book is printed on acid-free paper ∞

Manufactured in the United States of America

Contents

Series Foreword

All of us have questions about our health. Is this normal? Should I be doing something differently? Whom should I talk to about my concerns? And our modern world is full of answers. Thanks to the Internet, there's a wealth of information at our fingertips, from forums where people can share their personal experiences to Wikipedia articles to the full text of medical studies. But finding the right information can be an intimidating and difficult task—some sources are written at too high a level, others have been oversimplified, while still others are heavily biased or simply inaccurate.

Q&A Health Guides address the needs of readers who want accurate, concise answers to their health questions, authored by reputable and objective experts, and written in clear and easy-to-understand language. This series focuses on the topics that matter most to young adult readers, including various aspects of physical and emotional well-being as well as other components of a healthy lifestyle. These guides will also serve as a valuable tool for parents, school counselors, and others who may need to answer teens' health questions.

All books in the series follow the same format to make finding information quick and easy. Each volume begins with an essay on health literacy and why it is so important when it comes to gathering and evaluating health information. Next, the top five myths and misconceptions that surround the topic are dispelled. The heart of each guide is a collection of questions and answers, organized thematically. A selection of five case studies provides real-world examples to illuminate key concepts. Rounding out each volume are a directory of resources, glossary, and index.

It is our hope that the books in this series will not only provide valuable information but will also help guide readers toward a lifetime of healthy decision making.

Acknowledgments

Every therapist has a personal journey that brings them to and through this work. When we are at our best, mistakes and failures call us to a rigorous and sometimes painful odyssey of reflection, study, vulnerability, and accountability, which endows us with the strength and wisdom to rebuild our lives and serve others along the way. I could never have written this book without the influence of the people with whom I have connected, loved, fought, and learned. To my parents, my ex-partners, and many friends who believed in me, even if only for a while, thank you.

I could not be the person or the writer I am today without the privilege of parenting a remarkable young human. Thank you to my daughter, who inspires me every day just by being who she is.

My clients have taught me more than I can ever articulate. Thank you for giving me the honor of witnessing and supporting your journeys.

I feel tremendous gratitude toward Jim LaPierre, LCSW; Keith Young, LCPC; and Wally Fraser, LCPC, without whom this book would not exist, and with whom my personal growth and recovery has reached places I never thought possible. Thank you.

Introduction

The rest of this book offers insights and advice on keeping relationships healthy from the perspective of a clinical psychotherapist. However, writing about healthy relationships is silly without writing about love and the experience of falling in love, cultivating love, and nurturing love. And writing about love does not work if we don't get personal. If my bachelor's degree in English taught me anything, it's that the introduction is where we can get personal.

For me, to "love" is to choose to nurture a connection with a person, to offer them care, attention, loyalty, empowerment, and trust, among other things. If the worst relationships feature abuse, the best feature the opposite: mutual investment in one another, a culture of teamwork, and a commitment to challenge and aid the other person in their personal growth. This is not the same as "falling in love." To fall "in love" is to experience the beauty in another person and feel overwhelmed with awe and a desire to connect. This is a subjective phenomenon; it has nothing to do with any agreed-upon standards of attractiveness or any rational assessment of who would be a good match for me or who would treat me well. The first person I fell in love with as an adult would never have made the cover (or even a small square of one of the back pages) of any beauty magazines. She was sturdy, sarcastic, and struggling to keep her mind functional as waves of agony and terror from past abuse washed over her. We were both 20 years old and completely incapable of anything close to the ideals and practices described in this book. We got swept up in the experience of each other and made some hasty (but fortunately not life-altering) decisions, such as getting engaged. The relationship flamed out after about a year, and that's okay. It was a fantastic experience, and I would not change it.

There is beauty in everyone, but my expectations or preconceptions of what an intimate partner would present may blind me to seeing it in some people. That's not a bad thing—I doubt I would get anything done if I walked around all day feeling transfixed by everyone's beauty. But it means that in order to fall in love, I'll need some channels of connection that open my eyes to what's in front of me. In order for that love to blossom into a relationship, the experience needs to be mutual, and it needs to lead to a joint decision to nurture a connection. We must work if it's going to last. I will also need to do something that is pretty challenging for those of us who do not come from idyllic childhoods, which is to allow the other person's experience of my beauty to be real for them. This does not make me a narcissist; it makes me someone who has the decency not to refute someone else's reality. If another person reports being taken with my smile, or my eyes, or my way of talking to children, or my jawline, or my decision to write a book, it is not for me to agree or disagree that these features have quality. It is for me to celebrate the fact that we can find and revel in one another's beauty.

To put it another way, in order to truly fall in love and maximize the joy in doing so, I need to get out of the way. I need to keep my ego in check so that I don't insist that another person see me the way I see myself or the way I want to be seen. I also need to feed my ego so that my desperation for an identity or for proof that I am lovable does not lead me to turn someone into a savior rather than a person with whom I can share and celebrate love. I made that mistake multiple times. It led me into a 17-year marriage with an admirable and beautiful person who was never really a healthy match for me and who I never really "fell in love" with, but who offered me the attention and the existential meaning that I could use to prop up a fragile ego. Falling in love has no neediness to it. I do not need a magnificent mountain to be anything other than what it is or to validate me in any way. I can simply appreciate it for what it is. But the act of loving is different: to actively maintain a connection requires mutual investment and care. And it does not always end happily. There are no guarantees.

Occasionally, I wish that I could have prevented the pain I experienced in failed relationships. Part of me wishes I knew all the things in this book when I first met my ex-wife, but then I remember that I needed to learn them in my own way in order to be the person I am now. As much pain as I experienced in that relationship, it was all worth it, even though when it started, I was utterly ignorant of any of the kind of wisdom I want to impart in the ensuing pages. That relationship pushed me to grow, to learn how to attune to others, and to value and respect myself. I could not be the person I am without it and could certainly never have written a book like this.

When I think about who might want to read this book, I'm thinking of a person who wants to love and feel loved and who wants to remove the barriers and land mines that impair that type of connection. In reality, the lessons offered here will only sink in if they somehow resonate or connect with something the reader has experienced, even if those experiences were in platonic or family relationships rather than intimate partnerships. This book will not help you prevent every mistake, nor will it help you avoid the pain of losing love or being mistreated. I hope that the tools and insights offered here will help you feel optimistic and hopeful about love, and, most of all, open to it and be willing to see the beauty and nobility in people even if those people will sometimes hurt us. Relationships of all kinds (not just intimate partnerships) are worth maintaining, even if they are not perfectly healthy in every way and even if they don't last. They stretch and grow us, especially when we invest in them and work to improve them. As a person who has been through some hard breakups and painful losses, I can tell you that those experiences make those new experiences of love even sweeter.

Guide to Health Literacy

On her 13th birthday, Samantha was diagnosed with type 2 diabetes. She consulted her mom and her aunt, both of whom also have type 2 diabetes, and decided to go with their strategy of managing diabetes by taking insulin. As a result of participating in an after-school program at her middle school that focused on health literacy, she learned that she can help manage the level of glucose in her bloodstream by counting her carbohydrate intake, following a diabetic diet, and exercising regularly. But, what exactly should she do? How does she keep track of her carbohydrate intake? What is a diabetic diet? How long should she exercise and what type of exercise should she do? Samantha is a visual learner, so she turned to her favorite source of media, YouTube, to answer these questions. She found videos from individuals around the world sharing their experiences and tips, doctors (or at least people who have "Dr." in their YouTube channel names), government agencies such as the National Institutes of Health, and even video clips from cat lovers who have cats with diabetes. With guidance from the librarian and the health and science teachers at her school, she assessed the credibility of the information in these videos and even compared their suggestions to some of the print resources that she was able to find at her school library. Now, she knows exactly how to count her carbohydrate level, how to prepare and follow a diabetic diet, and how much (and what) exercise is needed daily. She intends to share her findings with her mom and her aunt, and now she wants to create a chart that summarizes what she has learned that she can share with her doctor.

Samantha's experience is not unique. She represents a shift in our society; an individual no longer views himself or herself as a passive recipient of medical care but as an active mediator of his or her own health. However, in this era when any individual can post his or her opinions and experiences with a particular health condition online with just a few clicks or publish a memoir, it is vital that people know how to assess the credibility of health information. Gone are the days when "publishing" health information required intense vetting. The health information landscape is highly saturated, and people have innumerable sources where they can find information about practically any health topic. The sources (whether print, online, or a person) that an individual consults for health information are crucial because the accuracy and trustworthiness of the information can potentially affect his or her overall health. The ability to find, select, assess, and use health information constitutes a type of literacy—health literacy—that everyone must possess.

THE DEFINITION AND PHASES OF HEALTH LITERACY

One of the most popular definitions for health literacy comes from Ratzan and Parker (2000), who describe health literacy as "the degree to which individuals have the capacity to obtain, process, and understand basic health information and services needed to make appropriate health decisions." Recent research has extrapolated health literacy into health literacy bits, further shedding light on the multiple phases and literacy practices that are embedded within the multifaceted concept of health literacy. Although this research has focused primarily on online health information seeking, these health literacy bits are needed to successfully navigate both print and online sources. There are six phases of health information seeking: (1) Information Need Identification and Question Formulation, (2) Information Search, (3) Information Comprehension, (4) Information Assessment, (5) Information Management, and (6) Information Use.

The first phase is the *information need identification and question formulation phase.* In this phase, one needs to be able to develop and refine a range of questions to frame one's search and understand relevant health terms. In the second phase, *information search,* one has to possess appropriate searching skills, such as using proper keywords and correct spelling in search terms, especially when using search engines and databases. It is also crucial to understand how search engines work (i.e., how search results are derived, what the order of the search results means, how to use the snippets that are provided in the search results list to select websites, and how to determine which listings are ads on a search engine results page). One also has to limit reliance on surface characteristics, such as the design of a website or a book (a website or book that appears to have a lot of information or looks aesthetically pleasant does not necessarily mean it has good information) and language used (a website or book that utilizes jargon, the keywords that one used to conduct the search, or the word "information" does not necessarily indicate it will have good information). The next phase is *information comprehension*, whereby one needs to have the ability to read, comprehend, and recall the information (including textual, numerical, and visual content) one has located from the books and/or online resources.

To assess the credibility of health information (*information assessment* phase), one needs to be able to evaluate information for accuracy, evaluate how current the information is (e.g., when a website was last updated or when a book was published), and evaluate the creators of the source—for example, examine site sponsors or type of sites (.com, .gov, .edu, or .org) or the author of a book (practicing doctor, a celebrity doctor, a patient of a specific disease, etc.) to determine the believability of the person/organization providing the information. Such credibility perceptions tend to become generalized, so they must be frequently reexamined (e.g., the belief that a specific news agency always has credible health information needs continuous vetting). One also needs to evaluate the credibility of the medium (e.g., television, Internet, radio, social media, and book) and evaluate—not just accept without questioning—others' claims regarding the validity of a site, book, or other specific source of information. At this stage, one has to "make sense of information gathered from diverse sources by identifying misconceptions, main and supporting ideas, conflicting information, point of view, and biases" (American Association of School Librarians [AASL], 2009, p. 13) and conclude which sources/information are valid and accurate by using conscious strategies rather than simply using intuitive judgments or "rules of thumb." This phase is the most challenging segment of health information seeking and serves as a determinant of success (or lack thereof) in the information-seeking process. The following section on Sources of Health Information further explains this phase.

The fifth phase is *information management*, whereby one has to organize information that has been gathered in some manner to ensure easy retrieval and use in the future. The last phase is *information use*, in which one will synthesize information found across various resources, draw conclusions, and locate the answer to his or her original question and/or the content that fulfills the information need. This phase also often involves implementation, such as using the information to solve a health problem; make health-related decisions; identify and engage in behaviors that will help a person to avoid health risks; share the health information found with family members and friends who may benefit from it; and advocate more broadly for personal, family, or community health.

THE IMPORTANCE OF HEALTH LITERACY

The conception of health has moved from a passive view (someone is either well or ill) to one that is more active and process based (someone is working toward preventing or managing disease). Hence, the dominant focus has shifted from doctors and treatments to patients and prevention, resulting in the need to strengthen our ability and confidence (as patients and consumers of health care) to look for, assess, understand, manage, share, adapt, and use health-related information. An individual's health literacy level has been found to predict his or her health status better than age, race, educational attainment, employment status, and income level (National Network of Libraries of Medicine, 2013). Greater health literacy also enables individuals to better communicate with health care providers such as doctors, nutritionists, and therapists, as they can pose more relevant, informed, and useful questions to health care providers. Another added advantage of greater health literacy is better informa-tion-seeking skills, not only for health but also in other domains, such as completing assignments for school.

SOURCES OF HEALTH INFORMATION: THE GOOD, THE BAD, AND THE IN-BETWEEN

For generations, doctors, nurses, nutritionists, health coaches, and other health professionals have been the trusted sources of health information. Additionally, researchers have found that young adults, when they have health-related questions, typically turn to a family member who has had firsthand experience with a health condition because of their family mem-ber's close proximity and because of their past experience with, and trust in, this individual. Expertise should be a core consideration when consult-ing a person, website, or book for health information. The credentials and background of the person or author and conflicting interests of the author (and his or her organization) must be checked and validated to ensure the likely credibility of the health information they are conveying. While books often have implied credibility because of the peer-review process involved, self-publishing has challenged this credibility, so qualifications of book authors should also be verified. When it comes to health information, currency of the source must also be examined. When examining health information/studies presented, pay attention to the exhaustiveness of research methods utilized to offer recommendations or conclusions. Small and nondiverse sample size is often—but not always—an indication of reduced credibility. Studies that confuse correlation with causation is another potential issue to watch for. Information seekers must also pay attention to the sponsors of the research studies. For example, if a study is sponsored by manufacturers of drug Y and the study recommends that drug Y is the best treatment to manage or cure a disease, this may indicate a lack of objectivity on the part of the researchers.

The Internet is rapidly becoming one of the main sources of health information. Online forums, news agencies, personal blogs, social media sites, pharmacy sites, and celebrity "doctors" are all offering medical and health information targeted to various types of people in regard to all types of diseases and symptoms. There are professional journalists, citizen journalists, hoaxers, and people paid to write fake health news on various sites that may appear to have a legitimate domain name and may even have authors who claim to have professional credentials, such as an MD. All these sites *may* offer useful information or information that appears to be useful and relevant; however, much of the information may be debatable and may fall into gray areas that require readers to discern credibility, reliability, and biases.

While broad recognition and acceptance of certain media, institutions, and people often serve as the most popular determining factors to assess credibility of health information among young people, keep in mind that there are legitimate Internet sites, databases, and books that publish health information and serve as sources of health information for doctors, other health sites, and members of the public. For example, MedlinePlus (https://medlineplus.gov) has trusted sources on over 975 diseases and conditions and presents the information in easy-to-understand language.

The chart here presents factors to consider when assessing credibility of health information. However, keep in mind that these factors function only as a guide and require continuous updating to keep abreast with the changes in the landscape of health information, information sources, and technologies.

The chart can serve as a guide; however, approaching a librarian about how one can go about assessing the credibility of both print and online health information is far more effective than using generic checklist-type tools. While librarians are not health experts, they can apply and teach patrons strategies to determine the credibility of health information.

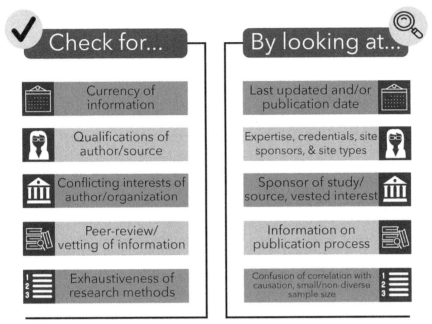

All images from flaticon.com

With the prevalence of fake sites and fake resources that appear to be legitimate, it is important to use the following health information assessment tips to verify health information that one has obtained (St. Jean et al., 2015, p. 151):

- **Don't assume you are right**: Even when you feel very sure about an answer, keep in mind that the answer may not be correct, and it is important to conduct (further) searches to validate the information.
- **Don't assume you are wrong**: You may actually have correct information, even if the information you encounter does not match—that is, you may be right and the resources that you have found may contain false information.
- **Take an open approach**: Maintain a critical stance by not including your preexisting beliefs as keywords (or letting them influence your choice of keywords) in a search, as this may influence what it is possible to find out.
- **Verify, verify, and verify**: Information found, especially on the Internet, needs to be validated, no matter how the information appears on the site (i.e., regardless of the appearance of the site or the quantity of information that is included).

Health literacy comes with experience navigating health information. Professional sources of health information, such as doctors, health care providers, and health databases, are still the best, but one also has the power to search for health information and then verify it by consulting with these trusted sources and by using the health information assessment tips and guide shared previously.

Mega Subramaniam, PhD
Associate Professor, College of Information Studies,
University of Maryland

REFERENCES AND FURTHER READING

American Association of School Librarians (AASL). (2009). *Standards for the 21st-century learner in action*. Chicago, IL: American Association of School Librarians.

Hilligoss, B., & Rieh, S.-Y. (2008). Developing a unifying framework of credibility assessment: Construct, heuristics, and interaction in context. *Information Processing & Management, 44*(4), 1467–1484.

Kuhlthau, C. C. (1988). Developing a model of the library search process: Cognitive and affective aspects. *Reference Quarterly, 28*(2), 232–242.

National Network of Libraries of Medicine (NNLM). (2013). Health literacy. Bethesda, MD: National Network of Libraries of Medicine. Retrieved from nnlm.gov/outreach/consumer/hlthlit.html

Ratzan, S. C., & Parker, R. M. (2000). Introduction. In C. R. Selden, M. Zorn, S. C. Ratzan, & R. M. Parker (Eds.), *National Library of Medicine current bibliographies in medicine: Health literacy*. NLM Pub. No. CBM 2000-1. Bethesda, MD: National Institutes of Health, U.S. Department of Health and Human Services.

St. Jean, B., Taylor, N. G., Kodama, C., & Subramaniam, M. (February 2017). Assessing the health information source perceptions of tweens using card-sorting exercises. *Journal of Information Science*. Retrieved from http://journals.sagepub.com/doi/abs/10.1177/0165551516687728

St. Jean, B., Subramaniam, M., Taylor, N. G., Follman, R., Kodama, C., & Casciotti, D. (2015). The influence of positive hypothesis testing on youths' online health-related information seeking. *New Library World, 116*(3/4), 136–154.

Subramaniam, M., St. Jean, B., Taylor, N. G., Kodama, C., Follman, R., & Casciotti, D. (2015). Bit by bit: Using design-based research to improve the health literacy of adolescents. *JMIR Research Protocols*,

4(2), paper e62. Retrieved from http://www.ncbi.nlm.nih.gov/pmc /articles/PMC4464334/

Valenza, J. (2016, November 26). Truth, truthiness, and triangulation: A news literacy toolkit for a "post-truth" world [Web log]. Retrieved from http://blogs.slj.com/neverendingsearch/2016/11/26/truth-truthiness -triangulation-and-the-librarian-way-a-news-literacy-toolkit-for-a -post-truth-world/

Common Misconceptions about Healthy Relationships

1. A HEALTHY RELATIONSHIP HAS LITTLE OR NO CONFLICT

Our attitudes toward conflict often reflect the culture of our family of origin. People who experienced conflict as chaotic or violent, as well as those who experienced little or no acknowledgment of conflict at all, are more likely to fear it. However, the healthiest relationships challenge both partners to grow into better versions of themselves. Professional athletes commonly talk about how good teams bring out the best in each player, but this result does not occur automatically. Only when teams have established a positive culture and a foundation of trust can "calling out" a teammate lead to better performance. Even those who have experienced conflict negatively can learn the skills to turn it into opportunities for growth. To learn more about healthy conflict resolution, see questions 32–40.

2. I AM NOT COMPLETE WITHOUT AN INTIMATE PARTNER RELATIONSHIP (AND I AM COMPLETE WITH ONE)

While "true love" is certainly a beautiful experience and well worth pursuing, your sweetheart (as wonderful as they may be) is probably not up to the task of providing all the experiences, values, beliefs, and memories a person needs to form a healthy identity. Furthermore, the pain of losing that relationship is intensely magnified if the relationship was functioning not only as a source of connection and intimacy, but also as your primary source of meaning and identity. As people mature, they come to realize that entering relationships as whole and confident human beings who do not need to depend on someone else's connection or approval to thrive helps them bring more to their relationships, thus making their relationships more satisfying and sustainable. Simply put, it is absolutely possible to have a complete identity and to lead a full and rewarding life without an intimate partnership; in fact, it is a very good idea to do so to the best of your ability until the right person comes along. Questions 1–3 address this point in more detail.

3. THERE IS SOMETHING WRONG IN THE RELATIONSHIP IF ONE OF US IS ATTRACTED TO SOMEONE ELSE

Here, it is important to note the distinction between "attraction" and "infatuation." Setting aside the roughly 5% of people in the United States who identify as polyamorous (more on polyamory in question 16), many people who are very happy in their monogamous relationships sometimes experience momentary and involuntary attraction to, or fantasies about, another person. This is normal; multiple surveys reliably indicate that about 70% of people in long-term relationships have experienced this. Refer to question 26 for more information on how to manage feelings of jealousy or conflict arising from a partner feeling attraction or infatuation outside the relationship.

4. INTIMATE PARTNER VIOLENCE CAN'T HAPPEN TO ME

About 25% of women and 14% of men in the United States will be victims of physical violence by a partner or spouse at some point in their lifetimes, according to the U.S. Centers for Disease Control and Prevention (CDC). The statistics are even worse for sexual violence, with about 33% of women and 17% of men being subjected to it at some point. Stereotypes would have us believe that most of these cases occur among the poor or uneducated or among victims with low self-esteem. While it is true that those of lower socioeconomic status are at slightly higher risk statistically, cases of intimate partner violence occur fairly evenly across income brackets. Privilege is not a reliable protector. For more on avoiding violence and abuse, see questions 26 and 27.

5. IN A SERIOUS DATING RELATIONSHIP, NOTHING SHOULD BE HIDDEN

It is often said that there should be "no secrets" in a healthy relationship. However, that does not mean there should be "no privacy." Understanding the distinction can save a lot of stress and conflict. While just about everyone agrees that trust is a key component in a healthy relationship, a person who wants no information hidden is sacrificing opportunities for trust. A person who is willing to say, "You don't have to tell me everything. I know you will tell me if there's something I need to know" is fostering a culture of trust in the relationship. For more on establishing healthy boundaries related to privacy, see question 24.

QUESTIONS AND ANSWERS

Dating and Attractiveness

1. How can I tell if I am ready to date or seek a partner?

Whether you've never dated before or you're recovering from a painful breakup, the question of when it is wise to find a partner occupies the minds of single people everywhere. Even if you'd rather not think about it, friends and family are likely to bring it up if they think you've gone too long without a committed relationship. Then there are those who would like to be in a relationship but don't trust themselves to choose the "right" person.

Being "ready" to seek a relationship does not mean a certain arbitrary amount of time has passed. It also does not mean the next person you choose will be your future husband or wife, nor does it mean you will choose so well that you won't experience pain, disappointment, or heartbreak. Being "ready" for a relationship means, you have a healthy mindset about what role the relationship would have in your life. Some relationships are just for companionship, while others include intense teamwork, focusing on the process of mutually working on a larger project, such as running a business or raising a family.

Some people seek relationships because they believe they are supposed to. Popular culture hypes dating and sex constantly. It may seem that you are surrounded by people who are either in a relationship or looking for one, so it's only natural to assume you should be doing the same. However, following these perceived expectations without an honest assessment of our own desires carries the risk of entering a relationship with compromised integrity (for the purposes of this book, "integrity" is defined as being at peace with oneself, such as by living in cohesion with one's values). Relationships tend to go poorly if one or both partners lack integrity.

Others seek relationships because they cannot tolerate loneliness (see question 2). Those who do not learn how to cope with (or maybe even enjoy) being single are more susceptible to manipulation or exploitation by a partner. The more desperate we feel, the more vulnerable we are, and the more likely we are to accept the first person who comes along who seems to like us. For many people, readiness for a relationship depends on readiness to do without one.

Preparing to find a good relationship requires two important ingredients: standards and social support.

Standards refer to the things you are willing to accept or not accept in your future partner or relationship experience. Many of us obsess over how we can be attractive or good enough for another person and forget to think about whether the other person is good enough for us. What would you need to see in the other person to determine that they would be a good companion and/or a good teammate?

Making a list of "must haves" and "can't stands" (a format employed by the dating service eHarmony) can be a helpful exercise. Here is an example:

MUST HAVES:

1. Has job
2. Is honest (willing to tell me things I don't want to hear)
3. Is easy to be honest with (reacts well when told things they don't want to hear)
4. Knows how to cook or is willing to learn
5. Has a good relationship with their parents
6. Good sense of humor—we find the same things funny
7. At least two shared interests/hobbies
8. Lives within 30-minute drive of me
9. Is physically attractive
10. Is liked by my friends

CAN'T STANDS:

1. Criminal record
2. History of violence

3. Substance abuse
4. History of cheating
5. Anxious or upset if I don't text more than twice a day
6. Drives recklessly
7. Has poor hygiene/smells bad
8. Criticizes/blames others for their problems

Your "must haves" and "can't stands" will depend somewhat on how serious or casual you want your next relationship to be: Do you see it lasting one night, a few weeks, a few months, or indefinitely (see question 7)? It can also be flexible depending on your underlying objectives. For example, maybe you put "criminal record" on your "can't stands" list because you want to ensure your personal safety, but you'd be willing to listen to someone's story to find out if they have learned from their history and are now safe. Such open-mindedness is laudable, but it requires rigorous honesty with oneself about whether we're "giving the benefit of the doubt" because they have met our standards or because we don't want to hurt their feelings or seem judgmental. (For more on standards and holding to them versus relaxing them, see question 38.) There are many "good people" who are not good partners. Using judgment in choosing a person to date is not the same as judging the person as inferior to you in some way. If you find yourself compromising something on your "must haves" or "can't stands" list, use a slow approach in building the relationship, and allow the other person to earn your trust over an extended period of time.

Social support is crucial for sustainable and satisfying relationships. Every relationship contains risks and rewards. If you have a strong network of friends and family who will be there for you when and if the relationship brings you pain, then you can enter a relationship with confidence that you will weather and grow from whatever problems or disappointments you experience. Also, when the relationship brings you joy, you will get to share and celebrate those experiences with these very same people.

If you have few friends or no friends and/or you have a poor relationship with your family, consider improving your overall social life before dating or seeking a relationship. This will improve both your relationship prospects and your likelihood of relationship satisfaction as you maintain connections with a network of people you love.

If you are already in a relationship but have few or no social connections outside of the relationship, it's not necessarily too late to build new friendships and new social opportunities for yourself. In a healthy relationship, this is something your partner would support (see question 22).

2. How do I cope with loneliness?

The internet circulates various memes pointing out that as humans, we must learn to feel okay being single so that we do not get attached to a substandard person out of desperation. A more positive view holds that alone time provides the chance to develop a healthier relationship with self. Once we reliably treat ourselves well, we come to expect others to treat us well. Plus, we develop the habits that enable us to feel fulfilled outside of a relationship so that when we do enter a relationship, we don't overburden it (see question 22).

Nineteenth-century essayist Ralph Waldo Emerson encouraged the pursuit of solitude. He distinguished "solitude" from "loneliness," or the condition of being alone, in that the former includes a connection to self and a connection to nature or spirituality that escapes us when we socialize. It is worth noting that Emerson considered production of or consumption of media, or even being surrounded by things created from human hands, to be forms of socializing. "To go into solitude," he wrote, "a [person] must retire as much from his chamber as from society. I am not solitary whilst I read and write, though nobody is with me. But if a [person] would be alone, let [them] look at the stars." A person who spends ample time connected to nature or beauty, Emerson argues, is a person who is well prepared to connect with others at a deeper, more meaningful level.

If Emerson were alive today, he would no doubt express concern at our level of dependence on technology and social media for cheap and convenient connection. For many people, social media breeds alienation because it shows us only airbrushed, sanitized highlights of people's lives, which the mind naturally compares to our own full range of experiences. Social media also brings us sensationalized and distorted representations of society on the principle that people are more likely to click on and react to content that is extreme. The mind naturally comes to regard this input as representative of reality, thus increasing a sense of danger and foreboding about the outside world that drives further isolation. Just when we are almost fully burned out by the threats, the algorithm shows us something or someone agreeable so that we can feel reassured. Thus, the computers hypnotically shift us back and forth between fear and comfort. A 2021 study by Common Sense Media (as reported by *USA Today*) found that 69% of young Black Americans and 67% of young Hispanic Americans encounter racist content online and in social media, while 74% of LGBTQ+ youth encounter homophobic content. Unsurprisingly, these findings correlate to higher rates of seeking mental health support via social media.

Clearly, scrolling is no answer for loneliness. Emerson's wisdom, translated into the language of a twenty-first-century mental health expert, tells us to either shift past loneliness into an experience of reverent solitude or to find genuine human connection that does not need to be romantic or sexual.

The next time you expect to be spending a day alone, imagine that a close friend's eight-year-old child has been left in your care. This child just happens to share your interests and tastes. It is important for you to care for this child as well as possible, which means planning a day that meets as many of the child's needs as possible—safety, healthy meals, exercise, stimulating learning opportunities, new experiences, and play, just to name a few. In order to ensure that your plans are meeting the child's needs, you check in with the child throughout the day to see how they are feeling (for example, maybe the child gets tired sooner than expected, which calls for plans to be adjusted to allow for some rest time). This communicates kindness and respect for the child's experience. Even if you decide not to alter plans to cater to the child's feelings, you would never simply barge forward with your planned day without listening to the child at all.

Suppose your plans materialize into cooking a big healthy breakfast, teaching the child to knit, and going on a hike. There is still room in the day for video games or a movie, but you prioritized some experiences that are both nurturing and engrossing. If the child has a sore tooth, then a dental appointment can be part of the day. If the child wants to experience some genuine human connection, it's time to set up a play date. Children naturally connect through play (as do adults, of course; more on this in question 12).

As you might guess, the idea here is to take care of yourself the same way you would take care of this child. Treat yourself to nurturing and fun experiences when you are alone. When you do socialize, prioritize genuine human connection, which in the adult world can take the form of play, but can also be experienced in real conversations with eye contact, sharing something creative or inspiring, or sharing meaningful or challenging experiences (see question 10). If your circle of friends and family does not afford you opportunities for such experiences, they can be found in churches, support groups, 12-step groups, and book clubs. And if you grow tired of the free options, you can always try therapy.

Even if your ultimate goal is to find a satisfying romantic relationship, your ability to demonstrate that you take good care of yourself will make you more attractive to any potential partner who isn't looking for someone to parent.

3. What can I do to be noticed by potential partners?

Many people use dating or hookup apps to meet people (see question 6). However, according to the Pew Research Center, only about 48% of 18- to 29-year-old Americans have ever used such apps, which suggests at least half of this demographic prefers to meet people in real life. While a dating profile may contain clues about body type, sense of humor, values, interests, and intelligence, it cannot reliably reveal one of the most important qualities for standing out from the crowd: confidence.

Confidence can best be defined as a belief in oneself and one's overall value and capability. If you pay attention, you can notice immediate physical and behavioral clues about a person's confidence. Posture, hygiene, eye contact (at least in Western cultures), and speaking with a full voice all indicate confidence. Research suggests that body positioning and behavior communicate calm to the brain's threat assessment systems, which means training yourself in these habits can lead to increased feelings of confidence. A 2012 study by Harvard social psychologist Amy Cuddy found that people who practiced "power poses"—standing or sitting in wide, tall, or aggressive-looking positions—experienced increased confidence and greater success in mock job interviews.

Clues about confidence also emerge when observing how a person treats others. Being a good listener demonstrates confidence because it shows a capacity to make room for others' viewpoints rather than elbowing them out of the way. Assertive communication (i.e., speaking clearly and directly about one's preferences or views without demeaning anyone) treats others with respect while maintaining integrity. An less confident person may either passively allow others to speak without offering anything substantial to the conversation or interrupt, talk over, or otherwise attempt to dominate the airspace to reduce the threat of someone else gaining attention with their ideas.

It can be difficult to distinguish confidence from narcissism or arrogance, both of which hide underlying insecurities. Rigidity can serve as an important sign of these. The *Tao Te Ching* compares confidence to water. It is "soft and yielding" but can carve mountains, which are supposedly strong and immovable. Rigid structures break under pressure; flexible structures bend and adapt. If you are able to accept that a person who challenges you is not a threat, you can adopt the posture of water. You can either flow around the disruption or flow over it, containing the influence and becoming bigger for it.

Easier said than done. Developing confidence requires more than the simple belief that you are not under threat. The mind changes through experience more than thought, which means developing genuine confidence requires the experience of success. Suppose someone asked you to walk across a room and open a door. How confident would you feel in completing this task? Most of us able-bodied adults would consider it an easy task because we have succeeded at it thousands of times. However, there was a time when this was not true. As small children, we struggled to stand upright, and then to remain upright while putting one foot in front of the other, and then more to work doorknobs. We had to fail at these tasks hundreds of times before finally succeeding, and then the sweetness of success—and the sweetness of knowing that perseverance can pay off—settled all the more powerfully into our minds after the grueling struggle.

In 2006, Stanford University professor Carol Dweck published a thunderously influential book called *Mindset*, in which she laid out a simple and efficient model of growing confidence. It involves shifting out of what she calls a "fixed mindset," in which we believe our skills, talents, and attributes (particularly intelligence) are innate and unchangeable, and into a "growth mindset," in which we see our skills, talents, and attributes as fluid. In the "fixed mindset," we view our performance as a perpetual quest to prove what we already have. In a "growth mindset," we perform in order to learn. Despite Dweck's growing popularity among educators, most of academia continues to reinforce the "fixed mindset" by rewarding students for constant strong performance. Under a "growth mindset," one could start the semester getting Fs and end the semester getting As or Bs, and one's learning could be celebrated. The only problem would be that the final average would be a C, which wouldn't impress many colleges.

What kind of world would we be living in if the valedictorians were the people who progressed the most rather than the people for whom school was relatively easy the whole time? For one thing, anxiety disorders among young people would plummet. A "fixed mindset" promotes anxiety because there is constant pressure to prove oneself. The idea of failure feels quite threatening because it prompts a questioning of one's identity and core value, opening the door for shame. Self-doubting thoughts like "maybe I'm not smart" are extremely common among students at whatever point they begin to find their coursework challenging, be it in kindergarten or graduate school. Shame feeds on the notion of inherent deficiency. Conversely, the "growth mindset" promotes confidence because all humans have the capacity to learn, and the more we experience and celebrate genuine learning, the more we reinforce for ourselves the idea that we can conquer future challenges.

The simplest and most powerful thing you can do to be noticed by high-quality potential partners is to boost your confidence, which means taking healthy risks, trying new things, and being willing to fail many times. If school is not a safe place for failure, then seek opportunities elsewhere. Take up cross-country skiing, read your poetry at open mic night, find a community action group or church where you can volunteer, or strike up a conversation with someone at a bus stop. These experiences, even if they go badly, foster self-respect and belief in oneself. Also, learning new things is only half the task. The other half is adjusting our attitudes about learning that is already taking place. Notice and celebrate the growth that is already happening, even if it seems insignificant. Learning to drive, learning to make omelets, or learning to change a diaper can all be viewed as either bland, expected tasks or as evidence of our capacity to develop skills and adapt to challenges.

People of all body types who respect and believe in themselves will generate interest from others. It is worth noting that people who lack confidence may still generate interest from some people, but consider who those potential partners would be. A person portraying low confidence through passivity will more likely attract someone with subconscious (or sometimes overt) desires to dominate and abuse. A person portraying low confidence through overcompensating aggressive behaviors will more likely attract someone who lacks the integrity necessary to sustain a healthy relationship.

4. How do I "ask someone out" without feeling awkward?

There are two main strategies here: let it be organic, and let it be awkward. First, let's discuss awkwardness. Usually when people say they feel "awkward," they mean some combination of clumsy, uncertain, and embarrassed. Many new experiences require a clumsy, uncertain, and embarrassing phase while we build skill and confidence, and initiating a conversation about the potential of dating is no exception. Unfortunately, various forms of media perpetuate the myth that only smooth and seductive overtures will elicit a favorable response, which can lead a person to give up before they've even tried. In reality, there is no need to allow the fear of awkwardness to prevent the effort. Ask someone out, even if you feel awkward. As discussed in question 3, genuine overall confidence and wholeness of self-esteem will likely show through even if you feel somewhat nervous in doing something for the first time. Furthermore, if you are expressing interest in someone who is similarly inexperienced, it would hardly be fair of them to judge.

Many people mitigate awkwardness by conducting these conversations over some sort of text messaging. This allows you to slow down and think about wording, but for some, it does not substantially eliminate nervousness or fear. Matching on a dating app provides some reassurance that there is mutual attraction, but that only gets you so far. One 2019 study from Norway found that only about half of Tinder users had ever met one of their matches in person, and about 80% had never experienced a sexual encounter as a result of using Tinder, even though it is widely known as a "hookup" app. Clearly, even with the help of dating app algorithms, most people find there are daunting hurdles to clear between matching and dating or sex. (More on dating and hookup apps will be covered in question 6.)

Sometimes people use the word "awkward" to refer to someone being inappropriate or creepy. Though there are some exceptions and variations depending on culture and context, here are some behaviors to avoid, as a general rule, when first initiating a conversation about going on a date:

- Commenting on a person's anatomy, especially body parts that are often associated with sexuality or that are not typically noticed (such as feet).
- Sending or requesting sexually explicit pictures.
- Expressing romantic or sexual interest in someone who is substantially younger or older than you.
- Expressing romantic or sexual interest in someone over whom you have authority or power (such as a supervisee in your workplace).
- Continuing to express romantic or sexual interest, or making flirtatious comments, after a person has declined, ignored, or politely redirected your overtures.

A solid strategy for fostering mutual interest in a dating relationship is "let it be organic," which means let it develop from natural circumstances. Pursue social experiences that interest you, such as clubs, classes, church groups, or community service. If you develop an interest in someone, invite them to participate in another experience that you would enjoy, or simply invite them to coffee or lunch. Repeated enjoyable experiences can lay the foundation for discussions about level of interest, attraction, and so on. (You can also use this strategy with a coworker, but be sure you are aware of any policies in your workplace regarding sexual harassment or relationships between coworkers.)

5. Will asking out a friend ruin the friendship?

A quick internet search reveals hundreds of stories of happy couples who started out as friends, but many people fear revealing romantic feelings to a friend, believing that if couplehood is not meant to be, the friendship might not survive. In reality, if the bond is close and the people involved are mature and mentally healthy, a friendship will likely withstand any difficult or awkward periods that come from revealing unrequited romantic interest.

In 2019, the *Washington Post* interviewed several dating experts about the pros and cons of exploring a romantic connection with a friend. Their analysis revealed some commonsense wisdom about when it could be the right move and how to maintain the friendship if the interest is not mutual.

First, assess if your friend meets your criteria for a desired partner (see question 1). Because you already know this person well, you have inside information about how well they treat past partners (not just how they've treated you as a friend), how honest they are, how they are with money, or other factors that may be important to you. Hopefully, you know that they are single (making a move on your friend while they are in a relationship with someone else definitely increases the risk of damage to the friendship, unless they identify as polyamorous or are practicing no-monogamy), and you know their attitudes about dating and relationships. Filtering your friend through your preestablished criteria can help you determine if your interest is legitimate, rather than connected to convenience.

Next, broach the topic in a direct but casual way. For example: "Sometimes I think we would make a good couple. What do you think about that?" or "I'm noticing that I'm starting to become more attracted to you. I don't want this to harm our friendship, but I feel like it's worth finding out if the feeling is mutual." Some may prefer a simpler approach: "I'd like to date you. How would you feel about that?" The experts interviewed by the *Post* mentioned the idea of inviting your friend to a "date-like" experience, such as dinner and a night out, to see if chemistry develops. Avoid initiating date-like experiences or physical contact without consent. Inviting a friend over to "hang out" and greeting them with flowers and a candlelit dinner might work well on TV, but in real life, it can feel like manipulation. Inviting your friend to a movie and then putting your hand on their leg could feel like a boundary crossing; even if your friend is attracted to you, they may prefer not to change the culture of the relationship without talking it over first.

Last, if your friend does not share your interest in dating or becoming a couple, continue to be a good friend. Let them know that you still want to be friends and that your life isn't ruined, even if you are disappointed by their answer. Treat them like you would want them to be treated by someone else. Respect the "no," and don't pressure, argue, or insist. This is one time when persistence does not pay off. They know your feelings and will let you know if theirs change. In the meantime, trust that if this is a truly valuable relationship in your life, the friendship is strong enough to weather one person's experience of catching unrequited feelings for a while.

6. Are dating or hookup apps a good way to meet potential partners?

A 2019 study by Stanford University sociologist Michael Rosenfeld found that people of all ages are now finding partners more through technology than through friends, family, or involvement in mutual interests. Whether this is a good thing or not depends on whom you ask.

Rosenfeld's study showed that meeting someone special online or in real life does not seem to matter in terms of predicting long-term relationship satisfaction. "Ultimately, it does not matter how you met your significant other," he told the *Stanford News*. "The relationship takes a life of its own after the initial meeting." On the other hand, John Birger, author of *Make Your Move: The New Science of Dating and Why Women Are in Charge*, makes a compelling case that couples who meet first in person are more likely to have a satisfying, long-term relationship. He cites research from Pace University suggesting that relationships that begin in real life last four times longer than those that begin online as well as a study from Illinois State University showing that younger adults are 25% more likely to report feelings of closeness to a partner if they first met in person.

These apparently contradictory findings result from the use of longevity as a metric of relationship satisfaction. Birger points out that the business model for most dating apps relies on repeat business, meaning they want to help you find a good dating experience, but not necessarily so good that you spend the next 30 years with that person. It is more profitable for Match Group (which owns Match, Tinder, OkCupid, Hinge, and Plenty of Fish) for you to have a decent short-term relationship and then come back and use their services again. This might seem cynical, Birger admitted in a 2021 article for *Newsweek*, but he says the evidence backs it up. For example, Hinge once had the best reputation for matching people into long-term relationships, with a model that prioritized setting up users with people already in their social circle. When Match Group bought Hinge, they did away with this method.

Then there is the dating app experience itself, which, various studies show, many people find frustrating. This likely reflects not only the turn-stile business models described above but also unrealistic expectations on the part of users. Dating apps purport to match people, which biases users to think some barriers to love have been removed. In fact, the experience of online dating offers just as many barriers as seeking a partner in person, if not more. The Pew Research Center found that 71% of dating app users think that it is "very common" for people to lie on their profiles, and more than half of females aged 18–34 have received unwanted sexually explicit images through dating apps and have had matches continue to try to contact them after they said they were no longer interested. Of course, people can lie to you or harass you in person, as well, but you don't need an academic study to know that people's behavior tends to be worse online. Plus, if your dating strategy focuses on meeting people in person, you can enjoy the fact that there are other ways to have a good time at most social events, even if it doesn't work out romantically.

Interestingly, the statistics about dating apps look different for those in the LGBTQ+ community. About twice as many people identifying as LGBTQ+ use dating apps, according to Pew, and 20% report having a long-term relationship as a result. Individuals in these demographics often feel they have fewer options for meeting people through more traditional means, especially in rural areas. They may also have less family or community support for finding a partner, as Rosenfeld points out.

As with most things, what you get out of using a dating app depends largely on what you put into it, and frustration level depends on managing expectations. A 2020 study published in the *Journal of Mental Health and Addiction* found that the problem of using dating apps most often correlated with sex-seeking and objectification or using the apps more to enhance self-esteem than to find a partner (i.e., building a profile designed to amass "likes" and to reassure one's self about attractiveness rather than to find a good match). Thus, it can be helpful to be honest with yourself about why you are using the app and what you are hoping for. If you want the next person you date to be the person you marry, you'll have better luck trying to forge relationships by joining community groups, going to social events, or asking a friend to recommend someone. If you're willing to accept (or maybe even prefer) that your next relationship may not be "the one," then swipe away.

When meeting people through any online platform, plan some rules for yourself to remain safe. Here are some suggestions:

1. Don't give out any personal information (address, phone number, financial information, etc.) to anyone until you've gotten to know them in person.
2. If you meet someone online who asks for money, do not comply. It is probably a scam.
3. If you match with someone and want to meet them in real life, do so in a public place, and/or bring a friend with you.
4. Some apps have a reputation as "hookup" apps. If you are not interested in a one-night-stand or "no strings attached" sexual encounter, make that clear in your profile.
5. Avoid matching with anyone who is significantly older or younger than you.

7. Is a "hookup" or "friends with benefits" arrangement right for me?

These terms, along with similar ones like "NSA" (no strings attached) and "ENM" (ethically nonmonogamous), are ambiguous. Different people may associate different types of physical intimacy with these terms. In some places, the term "hookup" simply means to meet somewhere. For the purposes of this book, the term "hookup" is defined as any sexual encounter (that may or may not include intercourse) without the expectation of any sort of continued relationship. The "benefits" in a "friends with benefits" arrangement is defined as any type of sexual activity without the expectation of a romantic partnership.

Deciding how to conduct one's sex life is a very personal choice. Often, we need to gain experience before we understand our sexuality enough to seek the most satisfying encounters. Some people find that having many different experiences with different people is a good way to learn. Others prefer to learn with a trusted partner or to learn alone, experimenting with fantasy and masturbation. Many people learn that they can feel arousal or attraction based on a variety of stimuli, such as physical appearance, movements, smells, behaviors, or situations. It can be very gratifying to experience all of the above along with an emotional connection, but some people find the most sexual satisfaction in encounters that lack emotional connection and focus mostly on physical pleasure.

Exploring sexuality with a committed partner brings the advantage of increased safety. The better we know someone, the easier it is to predict their behaviors, including whether they will respect boundaries and communicate honestly. You may find you prefer to have sexual experiences with a person you can trust to:

- Hear your sexual preferences or anxieties without judging or pressuring.
- Stop an activity when you ask them to.
- Give honest and authentic consent.
- Respect your privacy (i.e., not sharing details about or images from your sexual encounters with friends or in public forums).
- Respect your physical health (i.e., by disclosing any diseases or infections, being willing to use condoms, or by not acting violently).
- Communicate through check-ins before, throughout, or after the sexual experience.

If you are not particularly concerned about safety, you may feel more open to exploring your sexuality through hookups. While disregarding your safety can be a sign of low self-esteem (Why would we protect something that we do not value?), accepting certain types of risk can also be seen as a show of confidence in one's ability to cope with any problems that might occur. Take the time to assess if your choices reflect that you value and believe in yourself.

As you evaluate your own plans for sexual behaviors, it can be helpful to compare and contrast your attitudes and values to the surrounding culture. Casual sex is nothing new, but scholars have noticed a significant increase in the open expectations of casual sex, to the point where the term "hookup culture" has come into common use to describe the dominant attitudes and expectations around sex on many college campuses. In fact, multiple studies have demonstrated that young people engage in hookups, whether they like them or not, simply because they are not aware of any alternative. The culture places a premium on the autonomy that comes with enjoying sex without any sort of commitment. The emphasis on autonomy reflects a type of black-and-white thinking pervasive among young people, writes Conor Kelly in the *Journal of Feminist Studies in Religion*. People think you are either a free agent or you are smothered in a "joined at the hip" style of relationship. There is understandable fear that a relationship with too much connection or commitment can impede other social or academic development, but many teens as well as adults have yet to learn that a relationship with a moderate investment of emotional intimacy and connection can be part of a well-rounded life.

Hookup culture is fueled by substance abuse, most notably alcohol, which impairs people's inhibitions and decision-making. It is very common for drunk people to engage in sex acts they would not have chosen if they had been sober. A person cannot expect to behave in a sexually authentic way while under the influence. Sadly, it is quite common for people to agree to a "hookup" when it is not what they would authentically want, either because they are impaired or they want to be accepted and liked (or loved) or both. Despite many gains in gender equality, a double-standard persists in heteronormative environments; people identifying as female are far more likely to be judged or ridiculed both for eschewing sex when it is expected and for having a number of sexual partners. Although the ethos of hookup culture is freedom, often people find the social expectation to engage in casual sex feels too difficult to resist, especially when impaired and especially when feeling lonely (it can take some time to learn how to avoid feeling dehumanized or dehumanizing someone else; using a person sexually can stave off loneliness for a while, but it's not the same as forging a genuine connection). Also problematic are situations when a person enters into a committed relationship due to social pressures, when what they truly want is more independence or freedom to explore, experiment, or focus on other things. Then there are those who are naturally rebellious, doing the opposite of what they perceive to be expected of them, mainly for the sake of being different.

Your boundaries and expectations around sex are your own to choose. Negative sexual experiences are far less likely to result in trauma if you choose the experience with active awareness. In whatever way you conduct your sex life, you will do your mental health a big favor if you are choosing your experiences in a conscious and premeditated way, following your own desires, curiosity, and values rather than reacting to outside pressures or escaping emotions you'd rather not be feeling. Furthermore, healthy sexual interactions require understanding that each person involved is human, has feelings, and deserves respect. Whether you know them intimately or whether you know their name does not change that fact.

8. How do I keep the conversation going on a first date?

Rewarding conversations most often materialize when participants feel genuinely relaxed and confident. Sadly, this is far easier said than done for many people.

Anxiety and awkwardness in social situations, including dating, is quite common. According to the National Institute of Mental Health, about 7% of Americans meet the diagnostic criteria for Social Anxiety Disorder. Countless others feel the effects in ways that are less consistent, but still quite limiting. Often, the anxiety comes from feeling like people are watching or judging us, and any blemish, comment, or movement could be judged and criticized. Many of us find it helpful to remind ourselves that others are most likely too concerned with their own experience to be picking apart others or to remind ourselves that others' judgment is more a reflection on their character than a reason to self-examine. On a date, this translates to reminding ourselves that the other person is likely using up much attention on their own self-consciousness, and if they are actually being critical and judgmental, then it's probably not a person you want to be with, anyway.

Unfortunately, many people find these reminders unhelpful, because some forms of trauma manifest as social anxiety. It is common to hear people speak of having "social anxiety" as just being nervous around new people. In terms of an actual clinical diagnosis, it's a rather debilitating condition that is perhaps best described as situational posttraumatic stress. Around age 12, humans enter a phase of psychological development focused on establishing an identity, which includes having a way to fit in with others. Orientation to parents and other authority figures diminishes, and the urge to achieve social acceptance strengthens significantly. Sensitivity about this can last through the later teens (or longer if acceptance is a problem). Conveniently, this is also a period that features rapid and strange bodily changes, along with frequent and sudden shifts in peer social structures. In short, adolescents need not look very hard among their peers if they want to find peculiarities or eccentricities to criticize or mock as a means of achieving temporary relief from their own insecurities. Because the brain is in a particularly impressionable stage of development at this point, the wounds from bullying, or even from lower-key forms of rejection, can last a lifetime if unhealed. In fact, a 2015 study from the University of Warwick in the United Kingdom suggests that bullying can impair a person's long-term mental health more severely than child abuse or neglect. This likely results from the brain's high impressionability during adolescence, easily linking temporary characteristics (even if they are exaggerated) to a sense of permanent identity. Thus, we find adults who were called "fat" or "clumsy" or "smelly" continuing to feel insecurity about those issues well into adulthood and adults who felt they never knew the right thing to say to impress peers or potential dating partners continuing to struggle with anxiety in those areas.

Fortunately, several forms of psychotherapy have proven effective in treating social anxiety. Until you get around to doing that, here are some tips to try to smooth out and sustain conversations:

- *Start with small experiences.* If you are interested in getting to know one person in particular, try inviting them to a small gathering or activity with friends (such as a game night or helping someone move). This can help you get to know them a bit and provide some shared history, taking some of the pressure off that first one-on-one conversation.
- *Access your curiosity.* Ask a lot of open-ended questions of the other person. Getting them talking can take pressure off you to hold up the conversation. Some good questions include: Where did you grow up? Did you like it there? What's on your bucket list? What's your dream? What has dating been like for you? What are your friends like?
- *Seek areas of common interest or experience.* Ask about the other person's tastes and interest in music, art, movies, TV, books, and so on, and share yours.
- *Budget some attention to helping the other person feel comfortable.* They may be just as anxious as you are, or more!
- *Own your anxiety.* Sometimes setting the table for a more genuine and less superficial conversation can break the ice. At the very least, it communicates that you know you're not perfect and you're willing to do your best.
- *Yes, remind yourself that anxiety is usually irrational.* If it's a first date, you don't actually know how you're coming across to the other person. Change your negative "what ifs" to positive ones (e.g., "What if I say something awkward?" could become "What if they find my awkwardness endearing or cute?" and "What if I freeze up and can't think of something to say" can become "What if they don't like constant conversation and a stretch of quiet time feels comfortable to them?")

It is worth noting that many people rely on substances (mainly alcohol) to numb social anxiety. This is a risky strategy because (a) the substances impair decision-making, and (b) they do nothing to improve your social skills when sober, which means the substance comes to be relied upon chronically, drastically increasing the risk of developing chemical dependency or psychological addiction. Human history (and your local couples therapist's office) is littered with countless stories of people who coupled when drunk or high and then found themselves raising children without knowing how to talk to each other.

9. How do I respond to others who are pressuring me to date or become sexually active if I don't feel ready?

First, it is important to make clear that any form of pressure or coercion for sexual activity is unacceptable (see question 20). There are certain times when it is acceptable to persuade or encourage someone to do something they are reluctant to do: when you know a person well, genuinely care for their well-being, and have identified a strategy that could work for them in achieving their goals. Many people actually welcome being pushed under such circumstances, perhaps feeling that the pressure or encouragement can help them overcome fear and make a healthier choice. Pressuring someone into sex never falls into this category. Pressuring someone else into sex comes from a place of seeking one's own self-gratification or sense of control. Even if they genuinely care about the person overall, they are not acting that way when attempting to coerce or manipulate someone into a sexual encounter.

Choosing whether or not to engage in sexual activity or whether or not to date is a personal process. No one else's opinion deserves to supersede your own. Assessing if you are ready or not involves assessing your values, goals, and maturity. As with all forms of human connection, dating involves risk, and some risks may feel more intense or more consequential for some people. There is nothing wrong with deciding that you are not prepared to handle certain risks. Thinking through your boundaries and expectations ahead of time is the key to setting yourself up to follow through with choices that are right for you.

Popular culture portrays sexual activity, including intercourse, as a normal part of a dating relationship, maybe even on a first date. This seems to be an example of art imitating life. According to the Pew Research Center, 62% of American adults consider premarital sex acceptable at least some of the time. But that does not mean you should feel obligated to engage in sexual activity if you are not comfortable. In fact, there are numerous studies that suggest delaying sexual activity brings several benefits, including increased long-term viability of the partnership. Also, it is estimated that about 1% of the general population identifies as asexual, meaning they don't typically experience sexual attraction, though they may still have romantic feelings, interest in emotional intimacy, or occasional feelings of arousal. Those who identify as demisexual will only experience sexual attraction or urges once an emotional bond has been established, which may not occur until after two people have known each other for some time.

Many religious traditions discourage or forbid sexual intercourse and, in some cases, any type of sexual activity, before marriage. It is common for people to seek partners from the same religion in order to mitigate the chances of friction over sexual boundaries. However, even in relationships in which both partners wish to remain chaste before marriage, there may be disagreements about gray areas (what defines chastity, exactly) or failures to resist temptation. Learning and practicing effective communication skills about values and boundaries is the surest bet to prevent regrettable decisions.

If you feel you may be subject to pressure to engage in any type of activity (sexual or otherwise), it can be helpful to reflect on the people you choose to spend time with. Are the people in your life interested in your wellness and your growth, or are they more interested in how they can use you for their benefit? Reflect also on your background. Did your caregivers encourage your independence and create a structure in which you could make certain types of decisions for yourself? Or did they mostly make decisions for you? Are you used to following along with what others want, or do you see yourself as more of a leader, or as independent? Is it important to you to be liked, even if that means doing what you think others would want you to do so they will like you? Or are you willing to be disliked for the sake of maintaining your own integrity? If you answered these questions in a pattern that reveals a tendency to be passive, make a point of learning and practicing assertive communication skills (more on communication and conflict resolution in questions 31–40).

Coercion can sometimes sound innocent enough. Hearing statements like "You should start dating; you don't want to be alone the rest of your life" and "I just want to feel closer to you, and if we had sex I think it would bring us closer together" may not feel that harmful if you asked for the person's opinion as part of figuring out what you want, but in the context of you already stating what you want, they are a power-grab. The first example above can be answered with "This is the best choice for me right now" and the second with "There are many ways for us to feel close" (see question 11). Even if you don't have the sharpest answer, you can deliver your message effectively if you are committed to your values and boundaries. Practice saying no in the mirror. If politeness is important to you, practice saying "no, thank you" in the mirror. Both are complete sentences.

No one else is entitled to any form of satisfaction from what you do with your body or your social time. Allowing others to influence or control your experiences in a way that conflicts with your values or preferences is psychologically corrosive. Make a commitment that your mental health is worth standing up for. Other people are in your life temporarily. The only person you can most definitely never get away from is the one who looks at you in the mirror.

10. Does dating someone from a different background present any unique challenges?

Every relationship has its own unique challenges, many of which derive from the fact that each person in the relationship comes from a different background. Even if you date someone from the same town as you, your families are likely to have some different norms and values. It takes time to learn about each other's culture of origin. A healthy couple in a long-term committed relationship will respect and learn about each other's background, allowing space for each person to decide how much of their culture of origin they want to keep and how much they want to discard, collaborating on the formation of a new culture of the relationship.

The word "culture" can refer to a group's shared attitudes, beliefs, norms, values, or characteristics. Most people associate the word "culture" with geography or nationality. For example, it is reasonable to expect a person from Greece to identify with different characteristics than a person from Thailand, even if the two individuals do happen to have some traits in common. However, two individuals from the same country can exhibit cultural differences based on ethnicity, religion, economic class, population density (urban vs. rural), and education.

When differences are handled well, they can actually facilitate the strengthening of the bond between two people. University of San Diego Marriage and Family Therapy professor Lee Williams offers a helpful framework for this on his website "Two Churches, One Marriage." Dr. Williams recommends that couples take the time to learn about each other's religious beliefs and customs in a genuinely curious way (this approach can also be applied if one or both people are atheist or agnostic, as it is still possible to learn about the person's value system, what they believe gives life meaning, philosophical beliefs, and so on). This can be done by attending religious programming, reading, or having good conversations. Taking the initiative to learn on your own, rather than relying on your partner to teach you, is especially effective. "By learning more about our partner's faith, we are demonstrating in a concrete way that we value who our partner is and our desire to know them better," writes Williams. "This sends a powerful love message." It can also help to explore and emphasize areas of common ground, rather than focusing on differences.

Some couples fall into patterns of argument that sprout from expressing criticism or skepticism, which are thinly veiled attempts to gain or protect power. The best way to avoid problems is to refrain from trying to change or convert your partner. It can also help to feel secure enough in your beliefs that you do not feel like you have to defend them if they are attacked.

The good news about the above recommendations for handling religious differences is that they also apply to all other kinds of cultural differences. For example, if a person from Greece and a person from Thailand decide to date each other, they will do well to learn about the customs and traditions of each other's country, especially those that pertain to dating and relationships (i.e., What is considered flirting? What are the norms of public displays of affection? Do people date in groups or one-on-one?). They will do well not to pressure each other to acclimate to a culture other than their own and will take the time to identify and celebrate any common ground among Greek or Thai culture.

Contrasting norms and expectations related to socioeconomic background contribute to numerous challenges in relationships. People living in poverty have a much different relationship with authority, public institutions, and money, as well as different methods of conflict resolution and trust-building, than people who are steeped in middle-class culture (which tends toward greater trust in institutions like courts or schools) or wealth culture (which tends more toward using institutions for their advantage). While it is generally regarded as advantageous to have more money, that does not mean that one culture is superior to another, and it does not preclude a respectful exploration of the differences and commonalities present between two people from distinct socioeconomic origins. Again, the key is taking the time to learn about each other's culture and exploring commonalities while preserving the right for each person to decide what to keep and what to let go.

Open and respectful conversations about culture can help evade conflicts that result from power imbalances related to unequal status in the new relationship. Sometimes a person will give up much of their own culture and join a relationship in which elements of their partner's culture dominate. In this case, it can be said that one person is "immigrating" and the other is "native." A clear example of this is if the previous example of relationship between a Greek person and a Thai person takes place in Thailand. Naturally, the Greek person is the immigrant, and the Thai person has some built-in advantages and power in that situation. Other types of differences are harder to identify. For example, if Jae comes from a middle-class family and Bonita comes from poverty and the two of them live a middle-class lifestyle connected to middle-class friends, institutions, and expectations, then Bonita is essentially a cultural immigrant in the relationship. The couple will need to discuss how well she feels empowered to decide consciously what aspects of her culture she wants to let go and which ones she wants to retain, as well as in what ways she will need help acclimating to the new culture (assuming that's what she wants to do).

$$\diamondsuit$$

Building Connection and Trust

11. How can my partner and I feel more connected to each other?

Human beings form and strengthen bonds in three main ways: through shared experiences, trust-building, and play. This section will focus on shared experiences. Play and trust-building will be explored in questions 12 and 15, respectively.

The old expression "Nothing unites people like a common enemy" applies to the concept of bonding through shared experiences. Often, people who discuss intense, prolonged experiences, such as combat tours, say they feel a unique bond with those whom they served alongside, even the ones they don't like or would not prefer to spend time with in any other context. "If you weren't there, you wouldn't understand" is a common refrain among active-duty veterans when they describe barriers to seeking mental health supports (relatively few mental health professionals are veterans, and even those who are veterans frequently come from a different generation than the ones currently seeking help). Research indicates that losing the feeling of social connection and belonging during a transition back to civilian life is a significant exacerbator of posttraumatic stress disorder (PTSD) symptoms for combat veterans, which speaks to the importance of veterans connecting with one another. As far as they are concerned, if you *were* there, then you absolutely get it. No discussion is necessary to verify this.

Participants in 12-step recovery groups, such as Alcoholics Anonymous, experience a similar benefit as they work toward recovery. Addiction often comes with feelings of shame, but the most powerful antidotes to shame are connection and belonging. In recovery meetings, people can experience fellowship with those who understand the struggle from a first-hand perspective and have worked to attain sobriety and dignity.

In 2018, ESPN published a list of the best Hall of Fame induction speeches of all time, from all major professional sports. Almost every speech featured comments about parental sacrifices and important lessons from authority figures or spouses who supported them and pushed them to be better people, but these aging former athletes revealed some of the tightest bonds and fiercest loyalties in their comments about peers—most notably, siblings and teammates. Rarely were the individual strengths or qualities of these siblings or teammates featured in these speeches. Rather, the prevailing theme is simply that they were *there*. Of course, being there allowed for repeated experiences of trust-building and play, but the most powerful sentiment revolved around the sibling or teammates' merely bearing witness to, or participating in, the same challenges as the speaker.

A key ingredient for increasing the intensity of an experience is a shared challenge. Thus, one way to foster more of a bond in your relationship is to take on a difficult project together, such as traveling, volunteer work, starting a business, creating art, or raising a family. Shared experiences on a smaller scale, such as taking a martial arts class, going to an escape room, or trying a ropes course, can also be meaningful. Whatever the experience, a shared vision or goal enables it to be connective rather than alienating.

Thinking of your partner as a teammate can put you on track toward greater bonding, but, unfortunately, not everyone knows how to be a good teammate. Jon Gordon, leadership expert and best-selling author of the *Energy Bus*, consults with professional and collegiate teams at the highest levels, as well as Fortune 500 companies, about how to create a culture within teams that brings out the best in everybody involved. Gordon emphasizes the importance of every member of the team taking personal responsibility for bringing encouragement, optimism, and accountability to locker rooms, boardrooms, and lunchrooms. Gordon often emphasizes the "no complaining rule," under which teammates hold each other accountable for addressing problems in a constructive manner. His model does not ignore or sugarcoat problems and weaknesses, but it does wrap them in a context of resilience, confidence, and cooperative problem-solving. "Since a team will have to overcome the negative, they can't allow negativity from within to weaken them," writes Gordon in

2018's *The Power of a Positive Team*. "A positive team can withstand the negative forces coming at them, but they will crumble if the negativity comes from within. Positive teams know and believe that outside forces cannot truly defeat them. They can only defeat themselves." (Couples or families looking to conquer resentment or other gremlins of disconnection could do a lot worse than reading one of Jon Gordon's books for a sense of direction.)

Getting the most out of your shared experiences requires being a good teammate. Being a good teammate involves accepting some measure of leadership responsibility, and being an effective leader requires a spirit of service and mutuality rather than control. It also requires equanimity. Practice mindfulness skills and grounding techniques to help you remain calm in situations of conflict so that you can think clearly and convey a sense of reliability and self-control when others want to depend on you (see question 15 on building trust). Furthermore, practice viewing the people in your life in terms of their strengths and their value so that in moments of conflict or tension, you can rally together with belief in each other instead of pointing fingers.

12. Is it important that my partner and I have the same interests or hobbies?

In a Season 10 episode of *The Big Bang Theory*, Penny agrees to join Leonard at Comic-Con, despite her utter lack of interest in the event. Eventually, she admits she only wanted to go to support Leonard's passion. Leonard is relieved, because he was worried Penny would not enjoy the event. This conflict serves as a microcosm of what makes this TV relationship both intriguing and absurd: the characters share virtually no interests, but each exhibits a willingness to support the other in their own passions.

As explained previously, many strong attachments form during shared experiences. Those experiences do not have to be serious. According to Dr. Stuart Brown, MD, founder of the National Institute for Play, and author of the hugely influential book *Play: How It Shapes the Brain, Opens the Imagination, and Invigorates the Soul*, sometimes, our most meaningful and important bonds develop during activities that have no larger purpose or goal aside from in-the-moment enjoyment. For that reason, it is helpful for romantic partners to be able to enjoy *some* interests or hobbies together. It is not necessary for partners to always play together; in fact, it is most healthy for each person to devote time to fun pursuits outside the relationship. Different preferences regarding the exact balance of time together versus time apart commonly fuels conflict in relationships. A closer examination of Brown's work can reveal a useful framework for negotiating these concerns.

According to Brown, people play in a variety of ways but tend toward two or three dominant "play personalities." These are:

- Artist/creator: Takes a particular interest in visual arts and crafts, possibly enjoying a variety of media, such as drawing, painting, sculpting, woodworking, gardening, knitting, or machining. Those who love creative expression and those who love applying ingenuity or inventiveness both fit into this category.
- Collector: Likes to accumulate interesting or valuable objects and finds joy in organizing, showing, or simply owning them.
- Competitor: Finds excitement either in winning a competition or in maximizing their own effectiveness in an activity. The competitor's play experience may be direct or vicarious (i.e., being a fan).
- Director: Enjoys leadership roles, and planning and organizing events. A strong director may be adept at inspiring others and at creating structures in which others can find a niche and perform at their best.
- Explorer: Finds fun in exposing themselves to new places, experiences, or learning. An explorer may love to travel, try out new genres of fiction, or research new areas of interest.
- Joker: Delights in identifying and sharing or performing things that are funny, possibly earning a reputation as a "class clown."
- Kinesthete: Feels most at home and most gratified in movement. While an athlete may be a prime example of a kinesthete, competitive sports are not necessarily the focus of enjoyment. Kinesthetes are just as likely to develop a passion for dance, yoga, kayaking, and so on.
- Storyteller: Maximizes the potential of the imagination, immersing themselves in fiction or movies, challenging themselves to relate life events in entertaining ways or developing their own worlds and narratives. The storyteller could be considered an artist/creator who specializes in language.

The benefits of two people with the same dominant play style forming a couple are probably obvious. Remember that most people have more than one preferred play style, which means that it is actually pretty unlikely for two people to fully align. For example, a kinesthete/competitor and a kinesthete/joker may find some challenges enjoying a game of Ping-Pong together. With open and informed communication, couples can find creative ways to mix their play styles to maximize the potential of mutually enjoyable bonding activities. The Ping-Pong match can be played with high effort, but with moments of levity and teasing mixed in. Meanwhile, the kinesthete/competitor may also have a prized trading card collection they are planning to work on later in the day. Their partner has absolutely no interest in this and could be happy to spend that time meeting up with another friend to work on a comic book.

Responsible and productive adults, even if they grudgingly admit that play is important, often think of it as something secondary, something to set aside a little time for on weekends. Brown rejects this mindset, instead recommending that we infuse play into everything we do. Playful workers are productive workers. If we are parenting, do it playfully (Lawrence Cohen, PhD, wrote an exceptional book called *Playful Parenting*, if you are looking for even more reading material on what play does for trust and healthy attachments). In a romantic partnership, explore ways to merge play styles. For example, a trip to a national park can excite an explorer; if the explorer's partner is a storyteller they can take notes of important details or practice fun narratives about the discoveries.

Furthermore, supporting a partner in an activity that does not match your own play style can work if you find it rewarding to witness and encourage your partner in their own passion. At the same time, it would be unfair and unbalanced to expect this all the time. Eschewing an activity you don't enjoy so you can devote time to something more fulfilling for yourself is also a valid choice.

13. How can my partner and I learn to speak the same "love language?"

Gary Chapman's original book on *The Five Love Languages* first appeared in 1992. It has steadily gained influence, to the point where the term "love languages" is now common lexicon among couples therapists and laypersons alike. Chapman has written numerous follow-up books applying the concept across other types of relationships and environments, such as childhood, workplaces, and even the military.

As described by Chapman, the five love languages are acts of service, physical touch, words of affirmation, gifts, and quality time. Most people use all five but tend to have a favorite. Relationships can sour when people are not speaking the same love language. A person who receives love most through quality time may feel frustrated and neglected by a partner who is showering them with gifts rather than dates and road trips. The gift-giver may feel hurt and confused about why these expressions of love are falling flat. As a rule, couples can progress by translating for one another, intentionally expressing love in the other's language, or taking the time to notice when a partner expresses love in their language. The willingness to see the intent behind someone's words or actions is at least as useful as the effect of the translation itself.

If you are not sure what your love language is, Chapman's website, 5lovelanguages.com, has a quiz, along with some other helpful resources. Also, it can be helpful to think back on times in your childhood when you felt the most connected to, or loved by, your parents. Was it during a family vacation? During hugs or cuddle time? When receiving gifts? When receiving help with homework or with chores? When complimented, praised, or encouraged? Or perhaps one of these types of affection was missing, and you now find yourself particularly sensitive to it.

If you are not sure what your partner or friend's love language is, you can try delivering love using each of the five languages and see what seems to garner the most enthusiastic response. Of course, you can also start a conversation about it and ask them. Generally, the love languages are concrete and straightforward, with the exception of "words of affirmation" and "quality time," which benefit from a bit more discussion. "Affirmation" can be a tricky concept. Many people think of it as compliments or praise (i.e., "nice hat" or "you did a great job on your makeup this morning"). While these can be positive, they don't pack quite as much punch as encouragement. When we praise someone, we communicate approval of their actions based on our own values. When we encourage someone, we recognize their effort to connect with their own values and goals. In other words, praise is product oriented (assessing the result), and encouragement is process oriented (recognizing the effort). Praise is "Good job getting an A on your essay," and encouragement is "You must be proud that you got an A on your essay, you worked hard on it." The term "affirmation" speaks to recognizing a person's attempt to live in connection to their own goals, so "words of affirmation" as a love language will generate the most impact if you first take the time to understand a person's values and how their choices and actions seek to actualize them.

"Quality time" deserves special discussion for several reasons. Most people require healthy doses of it to feel connected and gratified in relationships, but it can look very different to different people. Playfulness is often a huge component of quality time, but people don't always like the same forms of play (as was discussed in question 12). People sometimes overlook the fact that time spent on separate pursuits while in proximity to one another might feel like "quality" time to one person, but the other person may be craving more of a shared experience. Sometimes, even a shared experience, like watching a movie, may not feel like quality time to certain people unless there is some level of conversation about it, during or after (in fact, conversation, especially conversation containing a certain level of intimate or vulnerable sharing, could be considered its own love language). For others, too much interaction actually reduces the quality of the shared experience. It can be challenging but worthwhile to find activities with the right style and quantity of interaction that feels rewarding to everyone involved.

People rarely think about love languages when a relationship is new. The excitement of a new connection seems to make everything feel natural. When relationships flounder over time, often, there is a failure to invest energy and effort in speaking and hearing a love language that is not the most comfortable. For example, if you are exhausting yourself with acts of service that seem to go unnoticed or unappreciated, it may be time to step back and reflect on how often your partner tries to reach out with physical touch or initiate date nights. A direct conversation about what each person finds gratifying can help pave the way for some new strategies, particularly in light of the fact that the most powerful use of certain "love languages" won't look exactly the same for any two people.

14. What are the barriers to connection, and how are they overcome?

During a recent speaking engagement, author Jon Gordon (whose work was referenced above in question 11) asked an audience of several hundred Division I student athletes if they knew what the opposite of fear is. Several answered with responses like "courage" or "determination" before he eventually enlightened the room: "The opposite of fear is love."

Anyone who has witnessed the effects of child or partner abuse can testify to this fact. It is difficult, if not impossible, to love a person we fear. Though many will try, the best they can really hope for is an experience of obsession or codependence that can easily be mistaken for love. On the other side of the coin, those who live in fear often become fearsome, resorting to power-hungry strategies to assuage their own anxiety rather than acting from a pure interest in the other person's wellness. One common example of this is the "helicopter parent"—a person whose imagination conjures images of horrible things happening to their children, thus leading them to supervise their children constantly. Ostensibly, this serves to protect the children, but in reality, it serves mainly to assuage the parent's anxiety at the expense of what the child actually needs. As children develop, they need some opportunities to experience the world without an adult within arm's reach.

Feeling unsafe can prompt several behaviors that undermine love. Psychologist John Gottman, one of the most influential and important figures in the history of couples therapy, became famous for developing a model through which he is able to predict with startling accuracy which marriages will end in divorce and which will last. He bases these predictions not on what issues people fight about, but on the frequency of certain toxic behaviors during conflict, which he calls the "four horsemen of the apocalypse":

- **Criticism.** Often taking the form of character assassination, criticism is easy to spot when it starts with a "you always" or "you never" (as in, "you always drink too much at parties" or "you never think about my needs, you only think about yourself"). Gottman is careful to distinguish criticism from complaints, which are more specific ("You said you would cook dinner, but it's 8:00 and you haven't started yet."). Both are negative, but at least, complaints can potentially be handled productively if they appear in moderation and don't trigger too much ego insecurity. People usually resort to criticism when they feel powerless to change their own feelings. Fearing they will remain trapped in a negative experience, they pressure the other person to change, with generalized language adding a sense of severity and urgency to a narrative of chronic victimization. In theory, it could elicit guilt or sympathy, followed by contrition and behavior change by the other person, but even in the rare cases when that works, it's still not a sustainable solution.

- **Defensiveness.** People frequently respond defensively in reaction to criticism or in reaction to complaints that feel like criticism. The objective is to combat the perceived threat of disconnection or disapproval by mounting an effective case for innocence. In the above example about not cooking dinner after promising to do so, a defensive reaction might sound like, "Look, I do a lot around here, okay? This place would fall apart without me." A defensive response may even include a counterattack, such as, "Maybe if I didn't have to pick up after you all the time, I'd have more time to tend to your culinary demands." Even without the counterattack, defensiveness serves to continue an adversarial courtroom dynamic where the parties exchange arguments in the vain hope that the other will suddenly realize how unfair they are being.

- **Contempt.** Gottman labels contempt as the most dangerous of the four horsemen. Language that ridicules, demeans, shames, or in some other way conveys an attitude of inherent superiority is the leading predictor of a doomed relationship. The example of contempt on the Gottman Institute website captures it best: "You're tired? Cry me a river. I've been with the kids all day, running around like mad to keep this house going, and all you do when you come home from work is flop down on that sofa like a child and play those idiotic video games. I don't have time to deal with another kid. Could you be any more pathetic?" Language that perpetuates a power differential by eroding another person's self-esteem can be seen as a response to fear (fear of losing control or fear related to unhealed trauma), or it can be seen as a cold, calculating means of dominating another person through shame. Either way, it constitutes emotional abuse and must not be tolerated.
- **Stonewalling.** When a person disengages or disappears from the conflict, perhaps by distracting, leaving, obsessing about other things, or simply ignoring their partner and remaining quiet, they are building a metaphorical stone wall to evade the conflict. A person who is stonewalling may be reacting to criticism or contempt, in which case this response is understandable but still not productive. It can be useful to view stonewalling as a sort of silent protest or as an expression of fear that continuing to engage will only make things worse.

To arrest the four horsemen, couples first need to be willing to identify and own their own behaviors and take responsibility for eliminating their own use of these tactics. Each person in the relationship must commit to turning away from fear and toward love, which means accepting some vulnerability and trusting that their partner will make an earnest effort to treat the vulnerability with kindness. Criticism can be translated into "I" statements that bridge toward cooperative problem-solving with each person's needs on the table. Defensiveness can be transformed by taking responsibility for one's mistakes or faults without a sense of general condemnation. Increasing a practice of encouragement, gratitude, and humility ("I'm not perfect, either") can stifle contempt. Stonewalling can be transformed into structured self-care—communicating the need for a break to calm down and gather one's self in order to reconnect with conflict management skills. Many people find that therapy can assist in achieving these improvements. A skilled therapist can not only help you remain accountable for changing your own patterns, they can also assist in healing and resolving underlying fears or trauma triggers that set the stage for the four horsemen in the first place.

15. How can my partner and I build trust?

As infants, we have no choice but to trust. We cry, and we trust that a nearby caregiver will provide the food or diaper change or eye contact or soothing that we need. As we grow, we continue to need caregivers to respond to our vulnerabilities with patient wisdom. A seven-year-old who punches a sibling needs an adult who will not only set and maintain a consistent standard of expectations and consequences for aggressive behavior, but who also recognizes the vulnerable emotions underneath that behavior and teaches (primarily by modeling) better ways of handling them. ("I can see that you were really angry at your sister for taking your bicycle. I think that would make me angry too, and I'm glad you didn't just let her get away with it, but in this family we handle our anger with words. Tell her how you feel and give her a chance to make it right, and if that doesn't work, come to me, and I'll help you.")

Most people can name a few commonsense ways to earn trust. Make eye contact, be consistent, and keep your word. All these things involve honoring what is vulnerable in another person: eye contact helps them know they are seen and that you care, consistency helps them know that it's important to you to be reliable, and keeping your word helps them know they can count on what you say and won't be left guessing when they need or want something from you.

In 2010, a social work researcher from Texas took the psychotherapy world by storm with a 20-minute TED Talk, titled "The Power of Vulnerability." Since then, Brené Brown has authored five *New York Times* Best Sellers; perhaps most notably 2015's *Daring Greatly*. The core finding of her research is that people who live gratifying, wholehearted lives accept that vulnerability is a necessary ingredient and that the healthiest and most satisfied people dare to trust themselves and others in new ways. Today it is hard to find a counselor in North America who is not aware of Brown's work.

Brown defines trust as "the act of making something important to you vulnerable to the actions of someone else." Note that trust and vulnerability go hand in hand. There is always an element of risk. Consider the hypothetical couple Eric and Lynette. Suppose Eric decides to disclose details of a new sexual fantasy to his partner, Lynette. Before doing so, Eric would do well to acknowledge to himself that he won't be able to predict Lynette's reaction with certainty. He is knowingly accepting some risk. In order to earn more trust, Lynette would respond with some form encouragement, even if she isn't interested in enacting the fantasy ("That's not something I'd like to do, but I'm glad we can talk to each other about these things" or "Wow, I never thought of that; what appeals to you about it?"). If Lynette responds to Eric's vulnerability with curiosity or kindness, and without judgment or repulsion, trust increases.

As explained in question 14, fear can impair our responses to someone else's vulnerability. If Lynette feels threatened in some way by Eric's fantasy (perhaps she anticipates feeling pressure or coercion, even if that's not Eric's intent), the odds that she will respond with one of the four horsemen increase substantially. This, in turn, reduces Eric's willingness to be vulnerable in other situations. Perhaps he decides not to share his sexual fantasies because he has experienced Lynnette's criticism of his cooking or her stonewalling his requests for more quality time. We can see how important it is for each member of a relationship to heal psychological wounds and handle their own fears well in order to increase the chances of responding well to vulnerability.

Handling one's own vulnerabilities kindly is a foundational practice. Do not expect others to respond with kindness and curiosity toward you if you are not willing to do the same for yourself. Being vulnerable with self in a healthy way means exploring one's emotions, moods, dreams, beliefs, thoughts, and impulses with a spirit of acceptance and interest. Self-talk that features criticism or contempt must be exchanged for self-talk that validates and encourages the fact that we are all humans and we all have our weird parts and our growth edges. Stonewalling of self, or becoming preoccupied with external stimuli and ignoring one's inner world, must also be curtailed. The practice of being responsibly vulnerable with self is akin to introspection, but with a specific attitude modeled after what a loving and wise caregiver would offer.

When a breach of trust has wounded a relationship, mishandling of vulnerability—especially vulnerability with self—is at the root. A partner who has been unfaithful likely failed to truly connect with and become accountable for pain they were experiencing in the relationship, setting the stage for subconscious sabotage of a toxic dynamic. An abusive partner may ignore wounds and allow rage to build unchecked, manifesting in behaviors of control and dehumanization that would be better directed at monsters from the past. A partner who fails to keep simple agreements like unloading the dishwasher may have failed to stop and assess their actual willingness to perform this task (your partner would prefer a direct no over a noncommittal "we'll see" or a "sure" that you may have uttered mainly to avoid a conflict in the moment). Responsible vulnerability with self is hard, if not impossible, to learn on your own. A qualified therapist can help guide these explorations until you feel more confident doing them independently.

One model for handling vulnerability with self was offered by Indiana University psychiatrist Stephen Porges, founder of the polyvagal theory, and his colleague, Deb Dana, author of *The Polyvagal Theory in Therapy*. The term "polyvagal" refers to the vagus nerve, which connects the brain stem to sensory nerves in the brain and to the stomach, diaphragm, heart, and lungs. This nerve is the highway of our autonomic nervous system, which assesses for safety and responds to perceived threats. The vagus nerve has two pathways, explains Dana: the ventral vagal pathway, which activates in situations of calm engagement and connection, and the dorsal vagal pathway, which responds to cues of danger. The dorsal vagal response impairs our reasoning and brings us toward a "fight, flight, or freeze" response. It triggers even in situations of social peril, when we may anticipate rejection or shame. A therapist trained in polyvagal theory will teach clients to assess where they are on the "autonomic ladder": in a ventral vagal state, we are "safe and social," but a perceived threat may bring us down the ladder to a mobilized, ready-to-fight-or-flee state of muscle tension or further down to a dorsal vagal state of immobilization or collapse. We learn to read our physiological responses to assess where we are on the "ladder" at any given moment and then plan interventions to help us climb back up to the "safe and social" zone or to more reliably remain there. Perhaps the most powerful result of this training comes from the social impact of the work; a partner (or anyone else in the room) is more likely to slip down the ladder if they see it happening to us and is more likely to remain "safe and social" if we do. In a relationship between equals, both people bear responsibility for maintaining or restoring calm in the dynamic.

If all this feels like an impossibly high standard of trustworthiness, the good news is that trust can be repaired even after hurtful responses. In the above example of Eric and Lynette, Lynette may have perceived a threat upon hearing about Eric's fantasies. Moving down the ladder to a "fight" response, she may have criticized or rejected Eric in the moment, but she can take the time to be vulnerable with herself and then revisit the topic after she has worked her way back up the polyvagal ladder: "I've been thinking about our conversation and I realized that my fear got in the way of my response. I felt that not being able to relate to your fantasy caused some distance between us that scared me. But I think it's more important to honor that you wanted to be close with me by sharing something personal and hoping we could connect over it."

16. Are monogamy and nonmonogamy equally healthy options for me?

For the purposes of this book, monogamy is defined as maintaining a sexual relationship with one person at a time. The overwhelming majority of relationships portrayed in popular culture have been monogamous, and monogamy is expected among those adhering to many of the predominant religious traditions around the world. However, research shows that nonmonogamous relationships are gaining popularity and are no less healthy or satisfying when practiced with consent, good communication, and transparency. A 2021 study out of Chapman University found that more than 10% of those surveyed in the United States and Canada said they had been polyamorous at some point in their lives, and nearly 12% identified ethical (consensual) nonmonogamy as their "ideal" relationship type. A 2018 University of Guelph study found that people practicing monogamy and consensual nonmonogamy experience the same levels of relationship satisfaction, psychological wellness, and sexual gratification.

It can be helpful to become familiar with more terminology. Generally, the term "open relationship" refers to an agreement to allow casual sexual relations with other people that exclude romantic feelings, whereas "polyamory" refers to allowing both sexual and romantic connections outside the relationship (a person being in love with more than one partner at a time). The term "swinging" refers to a couple pursuing outside sexual experiences together (i.e., swapping partners with another couple). The expectations, boundaries, and practices of nonmonogamy can vary considerably, but the enthusiastic and knowing consent of each person involved is the key ingredient to maintaining these practices in a healthy way (it is fair to point out that enthusiastic consent for sexual activities is no less important in monogamous relationships).

A person consenting to a nonmonogamous arrangement needs to have a healthy relationship with their emotions, especially jealousy (for more on jealousy, see question 25). Jealousy refers to a fear of losing the attention or affection of a loved one, coupled with negative feelings toward the perceived threat to attention or connection. Individuals who have experienced abandonment in childhood are particularly prone to intense feelings of jealousy. Jealousy, like any other emotion, is not itself unhealthy, but people sometimes make unhealthy choices in response to the feeling. A lot oft abusive or invasive behavior in relationships stems from jealousy because the jealous partner resorts to control tactics

to eradicate the fear of abandonment. For some people, a partner noticing another person or having sexual fantasies about another person feels
highly threatening, and they may label the same as "cheating." Others
feel secure in knowing that a partner's eye or imagination may wander
at times, but the bond runs far deeper than any of those behaviors can
affect. In polyamory, couples may feel little or no jealousy because they
feel confident that there is enough love to go around (similar to how a
child need not worry that their parents will love them less after a sibling is born). Other times, polyamorous people do feel jealous, in which
case they benefit from having healthy means to communicate their fears
and work together to establish expectations for boundaries and transparency that respect everyone involved. People in every kind of relationship
often find that secrecy is more likely to trigger jealousy than the actual
behavior that is being hidden, because sneaking itself indicates a lack of
trust. It can feel helpful to diffuse any sense of secrecy by expecting disclosure of details: with whom, where, and when sexual encounters take
place. Others find expectations of disclosure invasive and feel that there
is more trust communicated when there is no need for surveillance or
explanations. (It is worth noting once more that people in long-term
monogamous relationships experience just as many challenges on these
issues, though the specific boundaries or behaviors may vary. See question 24 for more about distinguishing secrecy from privacy.)

Generally, when people struggle in nonmonogamous relationships,
it is because they did not feel fully on board with the arrangement but
went along with it despite some misgivings. They may be afraid of being
rejected by the partner who more actively wanted nonmonogamy, or they
may have been in denial that they would feel jealous. At times, partners may agree to explore sexual experiences outside the relationship, but
one partner finds this more satisfying or easier to accomplish than the
other, which can breed feelings of resentment. If one partner wants sexual
experiences outside the relationship and the other cannot consent with
authenticity and enthusiasm, it may be a good idea to seek relationship
counseling to identify ways to compromise or explore alternatives.

Practicing monogamy or nonmonogamy is a personal choice. There is
no need to carry shame about either preference. In both practices, effective
and honest communication (with self and others) offers copious benefits.

Sexual Health

17. What are the ingredients of a healthy sex life?

Consent, respect, care, and authentic engagement make up the cornerstones of healthy sexual activity. All these require willingness to communicate honestly and with vulnerability.

Consent means everyone involved in the activity is freely, knowingly, and explicitly opting to participate. Consent requires that no one involved in the activity is coerced into it because they feel their options are limited or they don't know what is going on. Anyone is free to decline or stop an activity at any time, without repercussions. Partners are of legal age to give consent and are not experiencing impaired judgment from alcohol or other substances. The best sexual experiences occur when partners are not just willing to do it, but actively want to do it, and are communicating that desire with enthusiasm.

Respect means partners communicate about and honor boundaries, hopes, and expectations. Respect goes hand in hand with consent; partners have equal power, which means no one's decision-making is compromised by threats, manipulation, or substance use. When partners disagree about engaging in an activity (sexual or otherwise), the matter is discussed with a spirit of curiosity and mutual understanding, rather than with one person justifying their position and the other attempting to dismantle it to convince the other to give in. Furthermore, each person's body is treated as their own. Your partner's pleasure or orgasm is not a signifier of your "performance." Your partner's body and bodily responses are their own. You may facilitate the experience with their leadership (or impair the experience by crossing boundaries or exerting unwelcome control), but the amount of pleasure they have mainly reflects their own ability to be relaxed, present, and connected to their body and how it responds. (It is important to distinguish "pleasure" from "stimulation"—a person may experience physiological responses such as orgasm even if they are not experiencing pleasure and not wanting the experience.)

Care means that the partners think of each other as human beings rather than objects and are willing to consider what is best for the other person as well as themselves. Some people prefer sex partners they barely know and don't care about, because then they don't feel burdened by worrying about what the other person wants. Others feel that pleasing their partner is an immense priority and will neglect their own feelings or pleasure. Then there are those who think very little or not at all about the other person and focus on their own satisfaction. The healthiest and most gratifying experiences feature partners who are both tending to both people's preferences and needs.

Authentic engagement means being intentional about what you're doing and why, including assessing risks, and being present with the experience rather than dissociating, being mentally compromised by substances, or mired in doubt or anxiety. The many different kinds of sexual activity carry varying degrees of risk. Taking a healthy risk means compiling available information to weigh potential hazards against potential benefits and mitigating any unnecessary danger when possible. For example, the most dangerous thing the average American does in a given day is ride in a car. Millions of people are comfortable doing this because (a) convenient transportation brings a variety of benefits that make life fuller and more manageable and (b) measures can be taken to mitigate the risk, such as following traffic laws, wearing a seat belt, and so on. Even with all precautions in place, however, accidents still happen, which is why it is a good idea to feel comfortable and at peace with your decisions, factoring in your values, boundaries, and goals and proceeding with as little ambivalence as possible. (For more on how to reduce risks associated with sexual activity, see question 19. This section deals with sexual mindset and decision-making.)

Anyone who is or wants to become sexually active would do well to stop and consider their objectives in engaging in sexual activity. Are you hoping to experience more intimacy and connection with a partner? Are you hoping to become a parent? Are you curious about how something feels? Do you enjoy providing pleasure to someone you care about? Are you looking to relax or get your mind off something else? Are you afraid that your partner will reject you if you don't consent to sex? Do you feel a sense of control and power that you don't experience elsewhere? Are you simply doing what you think others expect you to do?

The most common reason people cite for choosing sexual activity is physical pleasure. It can be helpful to remember that pleasure may be experienced with or without orgasm. Many people think that orgasm is an essential component of sexual activity, if not the entire point. In a healthy sexual relationship, there is no pressure to orgasm. Partners emphasize simply enjoying the experience and doing what feels good. If orgasm is desired, one can take the time to explore the circumstances, fantasies, and body sensations that help make this possible. Though people commonly assume that intercourse is the most desirable and pleasurable form of sexual activity, this is not the case for everyone.

Below is a noncomprehensive list of activities that can be pleasurable but do not involve intercourse. When you have a firm sense of your goals and values regarding sexual activity, consider which of these apply:

- Snuggling
- Kissing
- Holding hands
- Flirting (smiling, winking, joking, use of innuendo, etc.)
- Dancing
- Massaging/caressing
- Stripping
- Showering together
- Fantasizing/sharing fantasies
- Grinding/humping
- Stimulating erogenous zones, such as earlobes, neck, lips, or nipples
- Masturbation
- Mutual masturbation (masturbating together)
- Masturbating a partner
- Sexual talk (compliments, discussing fantasies, etc.)
- Sexting
- Exchanging photos or images

"Intercourse" refers to a sexual activity that involves penetration or exchange of bodily fluids, namely:

- Fellatio (oral sex performed on a penis)
- Cunnilingus (oral sex performed on a vagina)

- Penile-vaginal intercourse
- Anal intercourse (typically a penis entering an anus)

Sometimes a person will say they are "abstaining from sex," but they really mean they are abstaining from intercourse. The behaviors in the first list may be in bounds. Moreover, a sexual relationship that focuses too much on intercourse and too little on nonintercourse activities is likely to be less satisfying. Wherever a person's boundaries are, respect them. Inviting them to describe the boundary with more precision or to share why the boundary is important to them is okay; mining for information so you can poke holes in their boundary and get what you want is *not* okay.

Many people are in the habit of subverting their own interests in order to serve others. Women are disproportionately conditioned to do so. "When women act in a more feminine, less confrontational way, we aren't being shy or stupid. We are being smart," writes Maria Konnikova in her 2020 best seller *The Biggest Bluff*, in which she describes her experiences climbing the ranks of professional poker players. "We are reacting to the realities of the world, knowing that to fail to do so is to incur potentially life-changing penalties." Konnikova describes how her awareness of this did not protect her from demuring to male poker players when she was a beginner. Early in her career, she found herself worrying about being liked or accepted at the expense of focusing on the best play, despite having told herself she would not. If it can happen at a poker table, it can most certainly happen in a bedroom. Thus, building one's overall confidence and practicing keeping commitments to self are important practices. Respecting boundaries and monitoring our urges to coerce, convince, or grab power in other ways is an even more important practice.

People who have experienced sexual trauma will sometimes use sex as a way of regaining a sense of power over what happened to them. A person who exhibits hypersexual tendencies may be very talented at pleasing partners and may even feel great satisfaction in doing so, without being in touch with themselves and their own pleasure or boundaries. The most rewarding and satisfying experiences of intimacy and connection (not just sexual ones) are possible when everyone involved can show up authentically, with a balance of attention to self and attention to the other person, rather than using the other person to compensate for unhealed trauma or insecurity.

Sadly, sexual violence is prevalent throughout the world. According to the U.S. CDC, 1 in 38 men and 1 in 5 women experience a completed or attempted rape at some point in their lives. Survivors of sexual violence can experience trauma triggers and other mental and physical challenges to enjoying a healthy sex life. If you have experienced sexual violence, please know that you are not alone and that a qualified therapist may be able to help you heal.

18. Are masturbation and pornography use healthy while in a relationship?

Masturbation, defined as the act of giving oneself sexual stimulation (usually by rubbing genitals with hands, fingers, or sex toys), is a normal and healthy activity. Medical experts agree that it is not only harmless, it provides several benefits, including stress relief, mood improvement, and relaxation. Generally, masturbation only becomes problematic when a person spends an inordinate amount of time on it (to the point where it disrupts other life goals or priorities) or when a person involves someone else without their empowered consent.

Sometimes people feel uncomfortable with masturbation in a relationship. However, while a partner may feel jealous of any sexual attention or efforts not directed toward them, there is no evidence to suggest that masturbating while in a relationship is unhealthy. "While some people believe there is no need for masturbation while in a relationship," writes sex therapist Matty Silver in a 2012 article for the *Sydney Morning Herald*, "self stimulation allows you to discover your own body and find out what you like. If you know your body and know what excites you then you can communicate that to your partner."

If you object to your partner having a solo sex life, it may be wise to reconsider your sense of boundaries. Your partner's body is their own. If you feel dissatisfied with the amount of sexual attention you receive from them, it may be tempting to blame masturbation, but chances are the two phenomena are unrelated. Many people have a strong enough libido to carry on a satisfying sexual relationship while also masturbating on a regular basis.

Use of pornography to aid in masturbation is quite common (studies consistently report between 70% and 90% of males and between 30% and 60% of females view pornography), but more controversial. It is important to acknowledge the ethical concerns related to pornography (its critics point out that the people depicted in sexually explicit images have often been exploited), but this section will focus more on its effects on individual sexual health and on relationship dynamics. As with masturbation, some consider the use of pornography while in a relationship to be a form of betrayal or cheating. Often, the more troubling culprit is the lack of transparency. A person who openly acknowledges their porn use from the start can be free of guilt from carrying on a habit behind their partner's back, but they also risk their partner feeling hurt or disgusted. Choosing not to disclose pornography use may result from carrying shame or from a desire to avoid conflict. It may also result from predicting that their partner's reaction could be harmful or distancing.

With the potential for such havoc in relationships related to pornography use, it is reasonable to ask why people don't just give it up for the sake of their partner. The allure of pornography is quite strong, primarily because it gives the user a feeling of control and ease that cannot be accessed with a real-life partner, points out Liza Featherstone in a 2005 article for *Psychology Today*. No matter what mood or interest you feel in the moment, there is a type of porn ready to satisfy it, and there is no need to consider another person's needs in the process. "What makes the woman in porn so erotic is not [how she looks], but the fact that she's 'crazy,'" says couples therapist Barry McCarthy, interviewed by Featherstone. "She's ever ready, always willing to do anything to please a man. No real woman could or would want to be that way." McCarthy notes that the real problems tend to arise when a person fails to differentiate pornography from reality and wonders why their real-life partner is not like the performers in the videos. As discussed above, many people are willing to accept masturbation or pornography use as part of their partner's sex life but are troubled by the hidden nature of it. It can be hard not to feel mistrusted if a partner chooses not to reveal this aspect of their sexuality.

What we view in the media tends to reflect what we feel is eluding us in real life. Just as those who like to watch sports may, deep down, be craving experiences of teamwork and competition, a person watching a certain type of porn may be experiencing a desire that can't be satisfied in real life (even if they have a loving partner, because no one person can satisfy every desire). Some pornography casts the viewer as powerful and dominant; other times, the viewer is nurtured and coddled. A real-life partner cannot be expected to adjust their own mood or sexual behaviors to suit any desire of the moment. A person watching explicit videos for the vicarious experience of feeling dominant (for example) may feel too embarrassed or ashamed to share this with a partner, even if the partner would be accepting. "Porn is never really the [core] issue," explains sexologist Claudia Six, also interviewed by *Psychology Today*. "It's usually erotic differences between the partners [that go uncommunicated]. . . . The secret use of porn is a symptom of the great sexual silence in many heterosexual relationships."

Whether you are in a relationship or not, pornography use does carry some risks, particularly for those who begin viewing it at a young age. Pornography can be addictive. Though pornography addiction can be difficult to define and quantify, the problems people experience mirror those experienced in other behavioral addictions or compulsions, such as gambling, according to a 2019 study published in the *Journal of Clinical Medicine*—namely, the need for increasing variety and quantity of exposure to achieve the same effects; sense of reliance upon the behavior to maintain functioning; and, in more severe cases, interference with other priorities, such as work or relationships. Those exhibiting signs of internet addiction are also more prone to struggles with executive functioning issues, such as impulsivity, decision-making, and emotion regulation.

Pornography can alter or shape sexual functioning. Gary Wilson, author of *Your Brain on Porn: Internet Pornography and the Emerging Science of Addiction*, points out that the more a person uses pornography before starting to have real-life sexual experiences, the more likely they are to experience problems having real-life sex, including low libido or inability to orgasm. Reported cases of erectile dysfunction in young men have skyrocketed in the internet porn era, according to the National Institutes of Health. Some people rely on pornography to the point where they are unable to feel aroused or sexually satisfied without it. A 2016 study published in the *Journal of Adolescent Medicine and Health* reported that 25% of high school seniors who regularly use pornography report abnormal sexual functioning.

The best advice regarding pornography from an individual mental health standpoint is to avoid use during adolescence and then use with moderation (if at all). From a relationship standpoint, open and respectful communication remains the primary protective factor.

19. How can I reduce the risks associated with sexual activity, including unwanted pregnancy and sexually transmitted infections?

The only 100% effective way to protect yourself from acquiring a sexually transmitted infection (STI) or from experiencing/facilitating an unwanted pregnancy is to abstain from sexual intercourse. As discussed under question 17 above, there are a variety of nonintercourse sexual activities that can be done with or without a partner that carry little or no risk of STI transmission or pregnancy. This section will provide information on the most common infections in the United States and discuss

Table 1 Common STIs

STI	Prevalence (total cases, new and existing)	Incidence (new cases, both diagnosed and undiagnosed)
HPV	42,500,000	13,000,000
HSV-2	18,600,000	572,000
Trichomoniasis	2,600,000	6,900,000
Chlamydia	2,400,000	4,000,000
HIV (ages 13+)	984,000	32,600
Gonorrhea	209,000	1,600,000
Syphilis (ages 14+)	156,000	146,000
HBV	103,000	8,300

Note: HBV, hepatitis B; HIV, human immunodeficiency virus; HPV, human papillomavirus; HSV-2, genital herpes; STI, sexually transmitted infection.

methods for mitigating risks during any of the three types of intercourse (penile-vaginal, penile-anal, and oral stimulation of genitals).

The U.S. CDC estimates that about 20% of the population is carrying an STI at any given time and that about half of new infections occur in those aged 15–24. Table 1, from the CDC, illustrates prevalence and incidence of the most common STIs as of 2022.

HPV, or human papillomavirus, is exceptionally common, in part, because it can be spread even by those who have no symptoms. In fact, a person may carry the virus for months or even years without knowing they have it. Often, the body's immune system kills off HPV without the need for any medical intervention. HPV is most commonly transmitted through penile-vaginal or penile-anal intercourse. Some forms of HPV can lead to what are commonly called "genital warts"—small, hard bumps that appear on or near the genitals. Contracting some types of HPV increases your risk of cancer (most commonly cervical cancer). Forms of HPV that cause cancer are not the same as those that cause genital warts. There is no test for HPV, but there is a vaccine available to boost immunity to it. The CDC recommends it for anyone between the ages of 11 and 26 (the vaccine is less effective for those over 26).

HSV-2, or genital herpes, is more common in women than in men. It is transmitted by skin-to-skin contact with a person who has a herpes sore or contact with secretions or fluids containing the virus. HSV-1 (oral herpes) may be transmitted to the genitals through touch or oral sex. As with

HPV, transmission of HSV-2 often occurs when the person carrying the virus does not show any symptoms and does not realize they are infected. Herpes sores can develop anywhere from 2 to 12 days after exposure, or not at all. Though there is no cure for herpes, serious complications are rare for adults with healthy immune systems. Stigma about herpes persists despite how common it is, which makes many people who may be carrying the virus reluctant to disclose this to potential partners.

Trichomoniasis results when a microscopic parasite called *trichomonas vaginalas* takes up residence inside the penis or the vagina. Only about 30% of infected persons will experience symptoms, usually itching or soreness in the genitals, painful urination, or discharge. Because so many people carry the microbe without experiencing symptoms, it is often passed to a partner unknowingly. Fortunately, trichomoniasis is curable with medication, and its primary complication is increasing the risk of acquiring or spreading other STIs.

Chlamydia can be spread to both men and women, but its complications for women are far more dire. Without treatment, chlamydia can permanently damage a woman's reproductive system, possibly rendering her unable to bear children. Men rarely experience complications from chlamydia. The most common symptoms are abnormal discharge, burning sensation when urinating, and (for men) testicular swelling. Chlamydia can also be spread to the rectum through anal sex, resulting in pain, bleeding, and discharge. Chlamydia can be detected with a laboratory test and is treatable with medication.

HIV, or human immunodeficiency virus, is most commonly known as the virus that causes AIDS (acquired immune deficiency syndrome), but those who receive treatment for HIV in its earlier stages may never develop AIDS. HIV attacks the body's immune system, making it harder to fend off other illnesses. A person may develop flu-like symptoms within two to four weeks of becoming infected, but some exhibit no symptoms. The only way to know for sure if you have it is to get tested. HIV is not only spread through unprotected sexual intercourse it is also spread through blood contact, such as sharing intravenous needles. According to the CDC, more than half of new infections result from male-to-male sexual contact. The other two most common forms of transmission are unprotected heterosexual contact and injection drug use. Chances of acquiring HIV increase if you already have another STI.

Gonorrhea, like chlamydia, most often manifests as abnormal discharge from the penis, vagina, or rectum; painful urination; and testicular swelling in men or nonmenstrual vaginal bleeding in women. Rectal infection can bring itching, soreness, bleeding, or painful bowel movements.

Unlike chlamydia, gonorrhea brings potentially serious complications for both men and women, including damage to the reproductive system, sterility, and long-term pain. In rare cases, the infection can spread to other parts of the body and become life threatening. Fortunately, gonorrhea can be cured with treatment by a medical provider, but the CDC says that strains that are resistant to antibiotics are becoming more prevalent.

Syphilis is diagnosed in stages. Primary syphilis shows up as usually painless sores around the site of infection, usually the genitals, rectum, or mouth. Secondary syphilis brings skin rash, sore lymph nodes, and fever. Then syphilis may enter a latent stage, in which there are no symptoms. This stage may last for years or decades, even without treatment. Sometimes, after anywhere from 10 to 30 years, the infection develops into a tertiary stage, which threatens major organs and can be fatal. Even when untreated, syphilis usually does not reach this stage. Syphilis can be treated with antibiotics. The CDC recommends regular testing for those living with HIV, those who have tested positive for syphilis in the past, and those who have male-to-male sexual contact, but any sexually active person can contract syphilis.

HBV, or hepatitis B, is a viral liver infection that can be spread through any exchange of bodily fluids, including unprotected sex. Newly infected people may not show symptoms; those who do can experience fatigue, poor appetite, abdominal pain, nausea, and jaundice (yellowing of the skin). About 25% of those infected in childhood and 15% of those infected in adulthood will die prematurely from liver problems. The CDC recommends vaccination against HBV for all infants.

Anyone who believes they may have been exposed to an STI would be wise to get tested by their medical provider or at a local family planning clinic. Most STIs carry risks of complications for unborn children, so anyone who may be pregnant or who may want to become pregnant needs to visit a doctor regularly for prenatal care and screening for possible STIs.

For those wishing to engage in sexual intercourse, using a latex condom or dental dam is the most common form of protection. When used consistently and correctly, latex barriers are nearly 100% effective at preventing transmission of most STIs (in cases of HPV and HSV, transmission is still likely if there is skin-to-skin contact on areas not covered by the barrier). "Consistently" means using one every time, through the entire sex act (the practice of "pulling out," or having unprotected sex but withdrawing the penis before ejaculation, is not effective at preventing most STI transmission or pregnancy, mainly due to the fact that most men emit a smaller amount of semen well before orgasm and some infections spread by bare skin contact more so than by fluid exchange). "Correctly" means checking to be sure the condom is not damaged or past its expiration date, placing the condom on the tip of the erect penis (taking care to be sure it is not inside out), pinching the end to provide a reservoir for semen, rolling the condom as far down as it will go, and withdrawing the penis immediately after ejaculation, while holding it at the base to ensure the condom does not slide off or spill. Using a water-based lubricant can help prevent the condom from breaking or tearing. Condoms are sold with instructions on the inside of the box. Use only one condom at a time, and never reuse condoms.

Some people prefer to use an internal condom, sometimes called a female condom. These are a bit less effective (about 95% effective at preventing the spread of STIs) and harder to use, but they cover more external surface area. Correct use involves squeezing the thicker inner ring together and pushing it inside the vagina, all the way up to the cervix. The larger outer ring remains outside the body and covers the labia. After intercourse, twist the outer ring, and remove it. For oral sex on a female, a thin, flat piece of latex commonly called a dental dam is very effective at preventing the spread of infection.

Condoms are also a reliable and widely trusted tool for preventing pregnancy. When used properly, they are effective about 99% of the time. Other common methods of contraception include:

- Birth control pills, which change a female's hormones to prevent ovulation and possibly menstruation (these are generally taken every day and require a prescription from a doctor).
- An intrauterine device (IUD), which a doctor installs in the uterus to hinder the fertilization of eggs or attachment of fertilized eggs to the uterine wall.
- An arm implant, injection, or patch (again, supplied by a doctor) that releases hormones with a similar effect as birth control pills only with longer effect, eliminating the need to remember to take a pill every day.
- A vaginal ring that also releases hormones that can prevent ovulation and menstruation.
- An emergency contraception or "morning after" pill, which is generally effective when taken as instructed but should not be relied upon as a primary method of contraception.
- Vasectomy, an outpatient surgical procedure in which the vas deferens is cut and cauterized, preventing sperm from traveling out of the testicles. A vasectomy is considered permanent; though it is possible to have a vasectomy reversed, success rates vary.

- Tubal ligation, a surgery that blocks fallopian tubes to prevent sperm encountering an egg. This procedure is considered permanent, though it may be reversible depending on the method of surgery. Tubal ligation is a less invasive and less involved procedure than vasectomy.

The contraception methods listed above are considered highly effective, but they all (except condoms and "morning after" pills) require a prescription or medical procedure. Often, people try to time their sexual intercourse, so it does not coincide with ovulation. This is commonly known as the "rhythm method" and is much less effective (out of every 100 women using this method exclusively, 24 will become pregnant). It can be difficult to track ovulation, and many women do not have regular menstrual cycles. Another common nonmedical method is withdrawal, which involves pulling the penis out of the vagina before ejaculation. This method is also not very effective, primarily because most men emit a smaller amount of semen a few moments before they orgasm, and because some men do not follow through with the "pulling out" plan reliably because they lack the bodily awareness or self-discipline to do so once they are enjoying intercourse.

It is important to stress that methods of preventing pregnancy do not necessarily prevent STIs.

Aside from the methods mentioned above, the most important steps for reducing risks associated with intercourse involve sound decision-making. Use of alcohol or other drugs, including cannabis, during or before sex is likely to increase impulsivity and reduce interest in, or effectiveness of, other precautions (good luck trying to use a condom correctly or talk coherently about your boundaries if you are drunk). Communicating with partners about their sexual history and whether they have practiced safe sex or been tested for STIs since their last possible exposure is a good idea. Those who practice monogamy (you and your partner agree to have sexual relations only with each other) are less likely to spread STIs than those who are nonmonogamous.

Given all the potential dangers and scary stories, some may find themselves wondering why anyone would ever want to engage in sexual intercourse (aside from trying for a pregnancy). Deciding whether the risks are worth the benefits is a personal choice. Many people find that intercourse increases feelings of intimacy and trust and is more pleasurable than other sexual activities. Some are simply curious, either to try it for the first time or to try it for the first time with a new partner. Regardless of your motives, it can be helpful to remember that sexual encounters of any kind can be enjoyable and worthwhile even if they don't look like what is portrayed in the media (magical and spontaneous, without any discussion of expectations or safety and without any mention of potential hazards).

20. What is sexual assault, and how can I avoid perpetrating it or becoming a victim of it?

Traditionally, most public education about sexual assault focuses on guiding people about how not to become victims. While this is sadly necessary, it implies that victims bear the responsibility of prevention, ignoring the need for perpetrators to be accountable for their actions. Significantly reducing the prevalence of sexual assault requires widespread commitment to actively learning to uproot the attitudes and beliefs that infect perpetrators who may otherwise seem to be "good" people. To say, "I didn't mean to" is not good enough. You have to mean not to.

Sexual assault is any sexual act that takes place without the consent of each person involved. The U.S. Department of Justice notes in its definition that this includes "when the victim lacks the capacity to consent" (most often because they are too young or are under the influence of alcohol or other drugs). Thus, the simple way to avoid committing a sexual assault is to make sure the other person is consenting. Unfortunately, the concept of consent is often misinterpreted. Below is a list of common misinterpretations or myths about consent:

- *Myth 1: A person wearing a revealing outfit is consenting to sexual contact.* This is false. A person can wear a revealing outfit because they like the way it looks, or because they like looking sexy. It is not necessarily because they are asking for a sexual experience.
- *Myth 2: A person who has agreed to go to your house or room after a date is consenting to sex.* This is false. Even though the media often portrays "going back to my place" as a euphemism for sexual activity, not everyone is on board with that expectation. A person may be unaware of the implication or may be interested in certain types of sexual activity but not others.
- *Myth 3: A person who is already engaged in kissing or intimate touching is consenting to more sexual contact or further sex acts.* This is false. A person may feel great about kissing, intimate touching, or any number of other acts, but that does not mean they feel great about any other act.
- *Myth 4: If I initiate a sex act and they don't say no explicitly, they are consenting.* This is false. Many people have trouble saying no when

they are uncomfortable, often because of fear of reprisal or because previous trauma history causes them to "freeze" or dissociate.

- *Myth 5: A person who says no may change their mind if I persist.* This is false. The vast majority of the time, a person who says no but then stops protesting if the perpetrator ignores their objection is assessing that fighting back or continuing to object would be more dangerous.
- *Myth 6: It is impossible to rape or sexually assault a male.* This is false. According to the CDC, one in three women and 1 in 4 men experience a completed or attempted sexual assault at some point during their life span. One in four girls and 1 in 13 boys experience sexual abuse in childhood.
- *Myth 7: A person who orgasms or has any other physiological response to the sexual contact has consented because they must have enjoyed the experience.* This is false. Erections, vaginal wetness, orgasms, or other physiological events represent the body's response to stimuli, not the mind's will or the heart's feelings. The body can respond this way even if the person has dissociated or if the person is feeling dehumanized.
- *Myth 8: A person who agrees to participate in a sex act has provided consent, no matter what the circumstances.* This is false. Consent by definition must be freely given. If a person agrees to something only because they feel under threat if they say no, then it's not consent. This may occur if there is a history or threat of violence or if the perpetrator has some power over the other person (i.e., can make decisions about their employment or influence their career). Also, a person may consent to a sex act but then change their mind part way through. Consent may be withdrawn.

In 2015, the Thames Valley Police Department in England published a short video featuring an explanation of consent that compared initiating sex to offering someone a cup of tea. The video has been widely copied and satirized, but the original can be found on YouTube and remains worth watching. Other sexuality educators at various colleges are comparing sex to the act of ordering a pizza with someone: you don't just order what you want and assume the other person will like it. You negotiate on toppings, when to order, where to order from, and so on. Some people like pineapple on pizza, others don't, and others will enjoy it occasionally, depending on mood. A person who liked vegetarian pizza last week may be more in the mood for breadsticks this week or perhaps nothing at all. Once the pizza arrives, a person can eat as much or as little as they want without judgment. Once a sexual activity begins, a person has the right to stop at any time they wish.

Ultimately, the most foolproof way to avoid committing a sexual assault (other than abstaining from sexual activity altogether) is to limit your sexual activities to people with whom you have discussed your mutual expectations and boundaries around sex. Many people find such conversations difficult or awkward, especially with people they don't know well. If this describes you, then it is probably a good idea to refrain from sexual activity with a person until you know them well and can trust their ability to be frank with you about their feelings. If you are not mature enough to discuss your feelings, expectations, and boundaries around sex and to listen to and respect someone else's, then you are probably not mature enough to be having sex.

Furthermore, it is a good idea to avoid using substances, especially alcohol. The National Institutes of Health estimates that about half of sexual assault cases involve the use of alcohol by the perpetrator, which is not surprising because it also stifles inhibitions and impairs judgment. Intoxication removes a person's ability to give consent, but it does not remove responsibility for one's actions.

It is commonly believed that protecting one's self from becoming a victim of sexual assault means not going out alone at night, carrying pepper spray, using the "buddy system" at parties, not drinking from an open container, and so on. While these steps make sense, they only account for attacks by strangers, which are actually much less common. Most people who become victims of sexual assault know their attacker. Often, the perpetrator is an intimate partner. To avoid becoming a victim of sexual assault, it can be helpful to work on overall assertiveness skills. Practice talking about your sexual expectations and boundaries, and practice saying no. Though it may feel awkward to do, rehearsing what you want to tell a partner about your boundaries and expectations can increase your likelihood of communicating well in the moment. Also, surround yourself with people who treat you with respect in general. The more you experience respect, the more you will come to expect it, and the more you will notice and respond accordingly when you are not getting it.

21. Who can I talk to about pregnancy, sex, or sexual health without others finding out?

Many teens and young adults have questions or concerns about sexual health but struggle to access trustworthy resources. It can be important to safeguard privacy from an intimate partner or from parents, either because of a general feeling of awkwardness or embarrassment or because there is a potential for experiencing abuse if certain people discover the sub-stance of those conversations. Fortunately, in the United States, privacy laws require medical and mental health professionals to safeguard the privacy of the people they serve. If you're under 18 or are not your own legal guardian, your parent or guardian can legally access your records. However, many providers will still keep your information private from a parent or guardian so that you feel more comfortable being honest and approaching them with questions. If you are 18 or over, medical and men-tal health practitioners cannot even acknowledge to others, even a parent or guardian, that you have visited them, unless you give them permission. However, if you are on your parents' health insurance plan, they may find out from the insurance company that a visit took place if it was billed to the insurance company.

Your primary care doctor is typically a good person to talk to about pregnancy or sexual health. A therapist or counselor is less likely to have training about physical health but can be a good resource to discuss healthy relationships and sexual practices. Both doctors and therapists are trained to assist others with these kinds of issues, so it is unlikely you will burden or embarrass them with your questions. If you don't have a primary care doctor or don't trust your doctor to handle your questions, contact your local family planning clinic (i.e., Planned Parenthood).

Often, young people turn to internet forums such as Reddit, or social media apps like TikTok, for answers to questions about sexuality or sexual health. It is important to remember that such forums or apps have no way to screen for the actual expertise of anyone who posts or answers questions. Even those who claim to have training may be exaggerating or misrepresenting themselves. Contacting a professional is a wiser choice. Even if they are not specifically trained in the issue that concerns you, they are more adept at connecting you to others who can help. Some states or Planned Parenthood agencies have anonymous hotlines that can also help.

If talking to a professional is not an option, see the resources section of this book for more reputable sources of information.

Healthy Boundaries

22. How can I avoid putting too much strain on my relationship?

Eli Finkel, professor of social psychology at Northwestern University, argues in his book *The All-or-Nothing Marriage* that expectations of intimate partnerships have changed over the last century or so. "We've added, on top of the expectation that we are going to love and cherish our spouse, the expectation that our spouse will help us grow, help us become a better version of ourselves," Finkel explained in a 2017 interview with the *Atlantic*. Many people, married or not, believe their partner should serve as a tool for their own self-actualization as well as be their primary source of emotional intimacy and support. This model of relationship was far less common a couple of generations ago.

Finkel argues that it is not necessarily unfair to ask so much of a relationship as long as you and your partner are explicit and consensual in these expectations, skilled at actually delivering what is promised, and are willing to offer as much as you hope to receive. Even so, leaning on one person for the bulk of your emotional and self-actualization needs requires a great deal of personal accountability (having the humility to examine honestly if what you want from your partner is also what you are giving) and constant work to adjust as the landscape of the relationship shifts with new life events, challenges, and growth experiences. Research suggests that it may be wiser to put a little less pressure on your intimate partnership. Accept that your partner may be terrific at offering certain types of support and may even be an excellent teammate for building a family but has other limitations.

As mentioned in question 1 of this book, maintaining a variety of social supports brings numerous benefits that help make a relationship more sustainable. Finkel cites a 2015 study from Northwestern University that found that people who rely on a "diverse portfolio" of friends and family (some who are good for sharing sadness, others who are good at giving advice, others who offer encouragement or help celebrate happiness, etc.) enjoy a higher quality of life than those who regularly connect with and receive support from a small number of people. While it is not necessarily unfair or unsustainable to expect a lot from your intimate partnership, people tend to feel disappointed if the partner is not capable or willing to meet those expectations. Even if they are, some fail to invest the time and work in the relationship that would help yield that type of return.

Renowned couples therapist John Gottman encourages people to strive for the "good enough relationship." Even if you are not attached to the idea of a love life that seems like a constant fairy tale, Gottman's message can seem disappointing at first glance. Upon further study, the "good enough relationship" is actually fairly challenging to attain for many people. "In a good enough relationship, people have high expectations for how they're treated. They expect to be treated with kindness, love, affection, and respect," explains Gottman. "They do not tolerate emotional or physical abuse. They expect their partner to be loyal." However, they also accept that conflict will be part of the picture and that a partner is not a magical source of peace and happiness. "It's unrealistic to expect a relationship to heal childhood wounds, or to become a pathway to spiritual enlightenment or self-actualization."

One way to reevaluate your expectations of a relationship is to study a model of human needs and note who helps you meet each need. The most famous of these is Abraham Maslow's hierarchy of human needs, first published in 1943. Countless psychologists and philosophers have adjusted and improved upon the concept of human needs. The Center for Nonviolent Communication offers a helpful needs inventory, reproduced in table 2.

For each need, write the name of at least two people who help you meet that need on a regular basis. If your intimate partner's name is the only one you can come up with for more than two or three of these or if their name is the first one you list for more than 75% of these needs, consider diversifying your social life. This can feel scary for some people. Allowing

Table 2 Needs Inventory

CONNECTION	PHYSICAL WELL-BEING	AUTONOMY
Acceptance	Air	Choice
Affection	Food	Freedom
Appreciation	Movement/exercise	Independence
Belonging	Rest/sleep	Space
Closeness	Safety	Spontaneity
Communication	Sexual expression	
Community	Shelter	**MEANING**
Companionship	Touch	Awareness
Compassion	Water	Celebration of life
Consideration		Challenge
Consistency		Clarity
Cooperation	**HONESTY**	Competence
Empathy	Authenticity	Consciousness
Inclusion	Integrity	Contribution
Intimacy	Presence	Creativity
Love		Discovery
Mutuality	**PLAY**	Effectiveness
Nurturing	Joy	Efficacy
Respect/self-respect	Humor	Growth
Safety		Hope
Security	**PEACE**	Learning
Stability	Beauty	Mourning
Support	Communion	Participation
To know and be known	Ease	Purpose
To see and be seen	Equality	Self-expression
To understand and to be understood	Harmony	Stimulation
Trust	Inspiration	To matter
Warmth	Order	Understanding

Source: Center for Nonviolent Communication — www.cnvc.org.

others to help meet more of our needs may feel like we are investing less in the relationship that is most important to us. Our partner may not enjoy feeling less needed. However, a relationship that is less codependent has a much better chance of long-term sustainability and satisfaction (see question 31 for more about codependency).

Some people refrain from seeking support from friends or family about stress in their relationship, perhaps because they want to avoid "airing their dirty laundry" or "talking behind their partner's back." But honoring a partner's privacy in this way comes with a price. It puts far more strain on the relationship. Consider how unrealistic it would be in any other context. For example, if you were having a conflict with your supervisor at work, it would be unreasonable to think you are only allowed to discuss that conflict with the supervisor and no one else. You may want to get advice from a friend, a union rep, and so on. A good supervisor would set aside any feelings of insecurity about this and recognize the necessity of people accessing other supports. In a healthy intimate partnership, each person understands the other's need to receive support regarding the relationship from other people. Trust your partner to assess who is safe to confide in and that when they receive support from others, it puts them in a better frame of mind for communicating with you about the issue when the time comes.

Perhaps the most important way to avoid putting too much strain on one's relationship is to recognize that you are in charge of meeting your own needs. Do not put a partner (or anyone else) in charge of meeting the needs for you. Though you may outsource some needs, you are ultimately responsible for all of them. If you do rely on someone to help you meet a need, don't allow yourself to be lost or helpless if something happens to them. Imagine that you own a house. Among the many needs a homeowner has is to keep the grass mowed. You can hire a landscaping company to take care of your lawn, and this may be a wise choice for you if you feel you have better things to do or if you want the job done professionally. But if the landscaping company calls you and says they are going out of business, you need to have a backup plan. If you have your own lawn mower and can do it yourself, that helps. Or you can access one of your many friends who can help you connect with a new landscaping company. For every need on the above list, it is important to have a way to take care of it on your own (or with a backup plan of your own making), even if you would generally prefer not to. This takes pressure off your partner, so they can make room for their own needs without having to worry that you will suffer if they can't be there for you 100% of the time.

23. How much contact or texting is healthy in a relationship?

Many misunderstandings and hurt feelings can be prevented through a simple discussion of each person's expectations and patterns related to communication and quality time. For example, Lucas has grown accustomed to hourly messaging with the people most important to him. He enters a relationship with Brent, who feels more comfortable with a check-in once a day, or even once every few days, but values more quality attention during face-to-face time. Brent may even feel frustrated that Lucas is responding to messages on his phone when they had agreed to spend quality time together. The most sensible solution is for the two of them to negotiate a compromise. Perhaps they will text more often than Brent would like and less often than Lucas would like, with some stipulations for a certain amount of non-screen time when they are together (for more about resolving conflicts, see question 34).

To develop self-awareness about how often you want contact with a significant other, it can be helpful to learn about attachment theory. In the late 1950s, British psychologist John Bowlby began publishing new ideas about how children develop anxiety, low confidence, and other problems that pertain to relationships. Based on studies of small children's interactions with their parents in diverse and unexpected situations, Bowlby formulated conclusions about how we learn to attach to one another based on the responsiveness of a primary caregiver in infancy and toddlerhood. A typically developing newborn needs pretty much constant attention and connection to the primary caregiver(s). At its best, the attention covers a wide range of physical (food, warmth, diaper changes) and emotional (eye contact, play, touch) needs. With time, the baby can begin to explore the world and gradually increase how much time they spend outside of connection with the primary caregiver(s), tolerating greater and greater intervals of going without needs getting met or learning to meet the needs themselves. As childhood progresses, school, activities, and sports occupy more and more time, but the primary caregiver remains the center of the child's universe, a constant tether, and safety net that enables confident exploration of the world. Even in adolescence, when many young people prefer to interact minimally with parents, seeing the primary caregiver at least a few minutes a day can maintain the psychological need for secure attachment.

Bowlby's ideas were considered a revolutionary challenge to psychoanalytic theories that dominated the field in the 1950s and 1960s, but today attachment theory is considered foundational to understanding not only what lies at the root of many childhood behavior problems, but also how we function in adult relationships, once a partner replaces a parent as our primary attachment figure. Researchers like Chris Fraley at the University of Illinois continue to study how childhood attachment styles transfer into adult relationships and what can be done to help people feel more secure. "People who are relatively secure in their romantic relationships are more likely to view their partner as being responsive to their needs which, in turn, has downstream consequences for satisfaction, investment, and commitment in their relationships," states Fraley on his website. "In short, secure attachment has the potential to help strengthen the commitment between partners and the satisfaction people experience in their relationships."

Building on Bowlby's work, psychologists have identified four attachment styles:

1. **Secure attachment** develops when a child's primary caregiver is predictable and reliable in their level of responsiveness to the child's needs. Physical needs like food and diaper changes, as well as emotional needs like connection exhibited through eye contact and play, are provided consistently and unconditionally. A person with a secure attachment style feels comfortable going off on their own to do other things, knowing the attachment figure will be available when they return. They experience relatively little anxiety or need to manipulate to win the attention of the primary attachment figure.

2. **Anxious-ambivalent attachment** occurs when the child receives care in an inconsistent or unpredictable way. The child may develop ways of commanding attention through manipulation. As adults, this attachment style manifests in patterns that may be considered needy, clingy, or controlling. A person may desire comfort from the attachment figure while simultaneously feeling angry with them for perceived abandonment, resulting in a "push-pull" behavior pattern (pushing a person away, but then pulling them in).

3. **Anxious-avoidant attachment** manifests as a person appearing apathetic to a connection with the primary attachment figure. A child developing this attachment style may be experiencing some level of neglect and has learned that there is no way of them communicating their needs effectively or manipulating to get a need met. Essentially, they have given up on manipulation or control strategies. Anger and jealousy are subdued, as the person resists feeling too much dependency on any one relationship and thus does not feel as threatened if that relationship seems to be in jeopardy.

4. **Disorganized attachment** is seen in children who suffered abuse or abandonment at the hands of their primary caregiver. The caregiver may have met other needs to varying degrees of consistency, thus fostering a sense of need and security, but the instances of abuse or abandonment also instill fear, leaving the child mired in an intense inner

conflict about whether to trust or control. Disorganized attachment is relatively rare and can manifest as conduct disorder in children or antisocial personality disorder later in life.

As you might expect, a person with an anxious-ambivalent attachment style will likely prefer frequent contact, while a person with an anxious-avoidant style will want to make sure they have their space. In either case, developing an explicit plan for availability and connection can help ease anxiety. Whatever frequency and quality of contact you agree on, make sure you both follow through with the plan. Keeping your word is crucial when it comes to reducing attachment anxiety.

There are no set rules for frequency of texting/messaging or even frequency of in-person visits. Many people find it helpful to follow a "no double texting" policy (don't send an additional text without having received a reply to the first one, unless there is some special urgency) to avoid seeming needy or invasive. But in addition to learning etiquette for online behavior and messaging, it can be useful to recall what you've learned about attachment theory. Ask yourself reflective questions like:

1. If the other person is taking longer than I hoped to respond to a message, am I able to cope and move on to other things while I wait? Or do I feel anxious? Why is it important for them to answer immediately? What is the emergency?
2. Am I prone to taking a lack of immediate response personally?
3. Do I send several different texts, or lengthy texts, before my partner has a chance to respond? Am I willing to consider my partner's experience of this behavior?
4. If I always (or almost always) answer texts immediately (even if they are not about emergencies or not timely), what motivates me to do that? Do I feel overwhelmed, anxious, or put on the spot when receiving a text, or several texts at once? Am I willing to explain this to my partner and advocate for a different format of communication?
5. Do I respect the vulnerability of the person sending a text? Or do I avoid responding to messages because there is something uncomfortable? Do I tell myself "I'll reply to that later" and then forget to do so? Where does the discomfort come from? How would I feel if someone did that to a message I sent?
6. If I prefer not to reply to texts immediately, or if I prefer not to communicate by text, am I willing to explain this to the other person and discuss other options for each of us getting what we are looking for?

7. Am I willing to text "I don't mind if you don't answer right away, but I would like to hear back when you have a chance"?
8. Am I willing to text "I can't talk right now, but I'll get back to you ASAP/when my shift is over/when I'm thinking more clearly/by tomorrow night"? (If someone is anxious to hear back from you, it can be helpful to offer a time line of when they can expect you to be ready to engage.)

Also, rather than focusing on frequency expectations, practice reminding yourself of the following healthy practices and attitudes:

1. When you send a text, you probably don't know what the other person is in the middle of doing, thinking, or feeling at that moment.
2. Even if they read your text, they may not feel they are in a position to respond right away.
3. You are not entitled to an immediate response, and it is unhealthy to assume the other person must drop any other priorities at the moment you want their attention.
4. If you give your number to someone and tell them it is okay to call or text, most people would consider it rude or disrespectful to not answer messages at all.
5. It is okay to tell someone you are not available. It can be helpful to tell them when you expect to be able to reconnect.
6. Following through on agreements about frequency/nature of contact is an important way to build trust in your relationship.
7. It is notoriously difficult to accurately interpret the intended tone of a text. If you don't feel good about a text you receive, it is okay to reply, "I'm not sure if I'm getting the right tone of your message; maybe we should talk about this by phone/when we see each other in person."
8. If someone accuses you of texting like an older person, think of it as a compliment. It probably means you are mature in your communication.

A person living a busy and fulfilling life will probably not be able to answer texts all the time. The natural structure of such a life limits availability for frequent engagement and demands some scheduling and planning. However, a person with a variety of work obligations, hobbies, close friendships, and other interests can be very gratifying to connect with. If the frequency of connection in your relationship is not what you would like it to be, hopefully the quality and depth of connection balances that out. If not, consider seeking counseling or other help on how to improve the connection, or consider a relationship change.

24. Is it healthy to keep secrets in a relationship?

Healthy relationships respect each person's right to privacy. It is not reasonable and not advisable to expect a partner to disclose every detail of their daily movements, conversations, thoughts, feelings, and so on. This can feel like living under constant surveillance and control. More importantly, allowing for privacy creates a way to let go of control and trust your partner to govern themselves in a way that will not cause harm. "Cultivating . . . trust requires millions of micro-risks that show us we are not foolish for being confident in our relationship," explains famous couples therapist Esther Perel, author of the best seller *Mating in Captivity*. (The topic of trust is explored in more depth under question 15.) Secrets, on the other hand, represent a betrayal of trust. Unless you are hoping to surprise someone with a gift, secrets are best avoided. Thus, it is crucial to be able to differentiate privacy from secrecy.

The most direct way to assess if something is a secret or if it is private is to ask the question "Does anyone else need to know, or have a right to know?" For example, many states have "sunshine laws" that specify when the public may or may not be excluded from government proceedings. If your local school board holds a meeting that is closed to the public, but they discuss budgetary matters and tax rates in the meeting, the meeting could be rightly labeled "secret" because it is generally accepted in representative democracy that the public has the right to access their elected officials' discussions about how to spend public money. However, if they are discussing a teacher's disciplinary record, the meeting could be correctly labeled "private," because laws in most places safeguard, except in extreme cases, the personnel records of public employees.

When you go to visit a doctor or a therapist or if you sign up for an account with an online vendor, you are usually asked to sign a document acknowledging that you understand their "privacy practices." This means they want you to know how they safeguard information about you that no one else legitimately needs to access, such as your medical records or credit card number. Information is kept "private" when there is a need to protect against someone acting irresponsibly or abusively with that information. You certainly would not want your credit card information leaked to the wrong person. Sadly, the same could be said of many medical or mental health diagnoses, because of stigma.

For a relationship example, "Miranda" has been having sexual fantasies lately about a coworker. Does her husband, "Joe," have a right or a need to know this information? Most reputable couples therapists would say no, especially if there is reason to suspect Joe would react abusively. Arguably, Joe has the right to know if there is some sort of threat to the marriage. If Miranda were having an affair, for example, or if she were simply feeling unsatisfied with the relationship and thinking seriously about divorcing, keeping those facts from Joe and allowing him to continue believing the relationship is fine would rightly be considered secrecy. But merely fantasizing about other people is not a threat to most healthy relationships (if the fantasizing gets out of hand or becomes a preoccupation, it is probably a symptom of some deeper problems in the relationship that need to be addressed, even if the fantasies themselves are not). If Miranda does not trust herself to avoid developing a more serious infatuation with the coworker, she may choose to tell her husband about the fantasies as a way of keeping herself accountable but does not have an obligation to tell him. Miranda would do well to remember that if Joe demands to know about her sexual fantasies, or if she does not trust him to handle his emotions well if he were to find out that she has fantasies that aren't about him, this would be a red flag. Meanwhile, Joe does well to avoid prying into parts of his wife's mind that she prefers not to discuss, thus trusting her to assess for herself what needs to be disclosed for the sake of the relationship.

Before disclosing information to someone, see if you can sense why they want the information. Are they seeking "power over" you or "power with" you? Do they want to relate to you? To build intimacy? Or do they want to pressure you to change, to conform to what they want or to "fix" you? Is it so they can ease their own anxiety about situations beyond their control? If your mind reading abilities are on the fritz, instead sense within yourself if you feel the topic is personal or if you feel at undue risk by disclosing things. You are not obligated to tell anyone something just because they want you to. Instead, trust yourself to assess if the other person has a right to, or a need for, the information.

Suppose that Miranda and Joe share finances and Joe impulsively spend an entire paycheck at a casino and then has to work overtime for the next two weeks to recover the money. He may decide not to tell Miranda and may even invent a cover story about the overtime because he wants to avoid her judgment or her anxious reaction. However, because Miranda's financial wellness is also affected, she does have the right to know how their joint funds are being spent. If Joe is demonstrating himself to be irresponsible with money, some tough conversations need to be had about how financial decisions are made or whether it is wise to continue having joint finances. She would be deprived of the chance to have those conversations if she never finds out about the expense. Joe may rationalize the secrecy by saying he does not want to upset his wife, but realistically, the decision to risk upsetting his wife was already made when he walked into the casino. He would do well to consider how much more upset she would justifiably be if she discovers the elaborate concealment of his actions on top of the missing paycheck. The more egregious breach of trust would be Joe's failure to properly assess what information needs to be shared between them.

The examples above illustrate that a key step in differentiating secrecy and privacy is assessing if someone is made more vulnerable by the act of information being hidden. In the first example, Joe may have a right to know if his wife is losing interest in the marriage, but that does not mean she needs to tell him about the fantasies specifically. If she is happy and devoted in the marriage, then there is no reason to bring up the topic at all (although some couples do enjoy sharing fantasies as a way of enriching their sex life). In the second example, Miranda not knowing about the missing money or about a weakness in Joe's decision-making about money robs her of a chance to protect her own financial wellness. Joe's secret needs to be brought to light, so he can be accountable for his actions and participate in planning for better choices in the future.

25. How can I effectively communicate and maintain healthy boundaries?

Suppose you have planted a new lawn and you want people to avoid walking on it so the grass has a chance to grow. You could communicate this in a multitude of ways. You could put up a sign that says, "Please Keep off the Grass." If people ignore or fail to see the sign, you could rope off the area. A rope sends a more noticeable message, but it's not much of a barrier to anyone who would much prefer to be treading upon your grass. The next option might be a chain-link fence or maybe a fence with some barbed wire on it, but even then, a determined person can find their way through. Maybe the problem is that people can see through the barrier to the inviting open space on the other side. So next you might build a tall wall.

Communicating interpersonal boundaries may be thought of in much the same way. It is helpful to start with the least obstructive method: communicating your boundary in a polite but assertive manner. This is akin to erecting the "Please Keep off the Grass" sign. Giving people a chance to respect your boundary voluntarily not only potentially saves you the energy and expense of more impenetrable methods it also creates the opportunity for trust. If people actually respect the sign and keep off your grass, your faith in humanity and your overall positive feelings for your community grow. If the sign doesn't work, you might wonder if it was noticeable enough. Communicating your boundary in a more firm manner (i.e., roping off the area) is the next step. This often includes an "if-then" statement, such as "If you don't keep off my grass, then I will be putting up a fence" or "If you continue to swear at me, then I will be leaving this conversation." (If using an "if-then" statement, it is crucial that you follow through with the stated consequence; otherwise, you're essentially inviting people to walk on your grass with impunity because they know you won't really do anything about it. Your boundary has the teeth of an average speed limit sign.) Eventually, if the boundary continues to be crossed, you may need to resort to more drastic measures, which often means disengaging from the relationship—refusing to see each other in person, blocking on texting or messaging apps, and so on.

A boundary only exists if it has been communicated explicitly. Consider this example: Derek is annoyed that his uncle keeps discussing politics at family gatherings. Derek confides in a friend, "I can't believe he is so terrible with boundaries. He should know that those topics are uncomfortable for everyone." His friend asks if anyone has asked him to stop, and Derek says, "No, it should just be common sense." Even if you agree with Derek's opinion of the rules of well-mannered conversation, it is unfair to expect everyone else to simply know these rules. After Derek's friend explains this to him, Derek decides to communicate a boundary. At the next family gathering, he says, "Let's please not discuss politics today." His uncle, previously not realizing that his missives were bothering anybody, agrees.

Abandoning a boundary is not always a bad choice, but it may be necessary to replace it with an internal boundary. In the above example of Derek, suppose his uncle disregards his request to avoid a political discussion and launches into a monologue about the latest election results. Derek may choose to defuse the tension with humor or simply ignore the comments, rather than reinforce his stated boundary. If he interprets his uncle as incapable of respecting the boundary (perhaps his uncle has some sort of developmental disability), he may feel more willing to tolerate the behavior and not take it personally. This would serve as an internal boundary for Derek, allowing him to treat his uncle's comments as though they were bouncing off an invisible shield and dropping harmlessly to the floor.

If the idea of an internal boundary doesn't work, doesn't feel right, or can't be done authentically (pretending to ignore someone is not the same as actually ignoring them), Derek can try an if-then statement, but only if he is prepared to follow through. "I'd like to talk about something else. If we don't change the subject, I'm going into the other room to play with the kids," he might say. His uncle stops temporarily, but after a few minutes, can't or won't stop himself interjecting one more snide comment about the president. Derek would do well to stick to his if-then statement and proceed with his plan to go to the other room. If his uncle follows him and continues to pursue the topic, Derek may find himself reevaluating his relationship with his uncle and his interest in attending future family events. Whatever the case may be, abandoning a boundary after issuing an if-then statement is more problematic, because it violates trust. Future if-then statements are less likely to be taken seriously by others or issued confidently by Derek.

Note that anger is a natural reaction to having one's boundaries disrespected—it can serve as an indicator of when you are being mistreated—but it is not necessary for communicating or enforcing a boundary. Anger may come from interpreting the reasons for the other person's actions, such as "People are so inconsiderate and lazy; they'll just cut across my lawn and ignore the sign because they don't care about other people's feelings." This type of mind reading only saps energy and attention from your boundary-setting. You don't need to know *why* someone is crossing your boundaries. Maybe they are inconsiderate and selfish, maybe they can't read your sign, or maybe they are five years old (literally or functionally) and haven't learned to control impulses. Deciphering if a person is unwilling or if they are unable to respect the boundary may help you assess their character or think of creative compromises or internal boundaries, but it does not help with communicating a boundary, which is best done calmly and firmly.

Setting a boundary is not the same as controlling someone else's behavior. It is common to hear people confuse the two. For example, if a person says, "I set a boundary and told him not to text with other women anymore," they are misusing the word "boundary." Boundaries have to do with managing your own experience, not managing how someone behaves toward other people. You are certainly welcome to state an expectation or a request that your partner not text other people, but your partner is free to decline and proceed as they will. In the example above, there is no reason for Derek to try to stop his uncle from talking about politics with anyone else. In the context of an intimate relationship, attempting to control or pressure someone to change their behavior toward other people does not work as well as trusting them to not do anything that would threaten your relationship (or moving on from the relationship if they are not trustworthy).

Boundaries can be selectively applied, depending on your relationships. What you decide to discuss with your therapist or your lawyer may differ from what you decide to discuss with your coworkers or your children.

You may feel comfortable hugging your parents and your partner, but not your boss. No one is entitled to cross a boundary just because the boundary didn't apply to someone else. A relationship that has no boundaries at all—no privacy, no limits of access, no respected and understood time apart—is definitely unhealthy.

26. How can I understand and manage jealousy?

Jealousy has a terrible reputation, but it is a natural human emotion and can serve a purpose, illuminating a path to understanding our values and needs. But when people handle jealousy poorly, it can destroy relationships. Other parts of this book, particularly questions 15 and 24, explore healthy mindsets for building trust, a long-term strategy for countering the fear that fuels jealousy. This section will explain how to identify jealousy and practice in-the-moment short-term strategies for coping with it.

People often use the term "jealousy" interchangeably with "envy," but they are different experiences. Envy refers to the experience of wanting something another person has. Often people say things like "You got to go to Disney World on vacation? I'm so jealous," but technically, they are describing envy. Jealousy is the experience of fearing something being taken away from you. Many people first experience jealousy in childhood, when a new baby sibling is born. The older child might envy the attention being lavished upon the baby but may also feel jealous of the baby, fearing they are being replaced in the hearts of their parents.

Usually a person feels jealousy toward another person, but jealousy can be felt about anything that feels like a threat to an interpersonal connection that you value. For example, if your partner is spending more and more time playing video games, it is possible to feel jealous of the video games if you perceive that they could be replacing you to some degree.

The most common, yet least helpful, methods for coping with jealousy are seeking reassurance and seeking control. A jealous person may frequently or incessantly ask their partner to reiterate verbal assurances that there is no threat (seeking reassurance occasionally is fine; it only becomes a problem if you are relying on external assurances as your sole way of coping with jealousy). Or a person may attempt to convince or pressure someone to disengage with the perceived threat. In more severe situations, this manifests as actual monitoring or policing of the partner's activities. Consider the fictional couple Sandra and James. Sandra has made a friend at work named Simon and reveals to James that they have been having lunch together. If James has not yet learned healthy ways to manage jealousy, we may see him asking Sandra to repeat reassurances to him that she does not have feelings for Simon. If James is living with more dire levels of insecurity, he may pursue control and coercion strategies, such as trying to forbid Sandra from eating lunch with him, reading through her messages to find out more about her interactions with Simon, threatening her with violence if he catches her talking to him, and so on. Sandra may feel like she has to hide her interactions with Simon to avoid James's anger, even if there is nothing wrong with what she is doing. If James discovers anything hidden or lied about, he treats that as further evidence that his jealousy is warranted.

A person who is prone to reassurance-seeking or control strategies in response to jealousy may need help from a mental health professional to correct these patterns. Often, a therapist will encourage the development of a mindfulness practice, wherein a person practices observing their emotions and thoughts without reacting to them. As a person gains more and more proclivity in observing their inner experiences, they gain the capability to choose different responses to their emotions, such as self-reassurance rather than demanding reassurance from others. If you lack the resources to get help from a therapist, consider learning more about mindfulness or meditation on your own. YouTube has many videos for beginners that can explain or guide you through the practice.

Returning to the above example, if James feels jealous, but has devoted himself to a mindfulness practice and to learning how to respond to his feelings, he is more likely to curb initial impulses to control the situation and to instead treat the jealousy as a sign that he is feeling some fear. He can ask himself if the fear is founded or unfounded. If the fear is unfounded, meaning objective evidence points to there being nothing to worry about, James can respond to the fear by reassuring himself with the facts. "We've been on two dates in the past week, and both had a great time. I've felt like she is present and connected during our time together. Plus, I've decided that she has good character and that I can trust her; otherwise, I would not be dating her." But perhaps James feels his fears are at least somewhat founded—that the quality of their connection has been eroding or that he is feeling more distance between them lately. In that case, he would do well to discuss his concerns with Sandra directly and invite her to join him in increasing efforts to nurture the relationship. He might say something like "I've noticed myself feeling jealous of Simon. I want you to know that I trust you and that you deserve to have whatever friends you feel are good for you. But I do feel like my jealousy is related to feeling less connected to you lately. I'd like us to talk about some positive ways we can feel closer." Even in the worst-case scenario—that James's

Table 3 ABC Worksheet

Antecedent event	Belief (interpretation of the event)	Consequence (emotion)	Wiser self-talk
Sandra is texting on her phone again. I wonder if she is texting Simon.	Simon is encroaching on my relationship with Sandra. She would rather text him than spend time with me.	Jealousy/ panic/ freaking out	I can trust my assessment of Sandra's character, and I know she is trustworthy. She could be texting anyone, and it's really none of my business. But I would like to feel more connected to her, and there are ways to accomplish that.

fears are fully realistic and Sandra has been harboring a serious desire to end her relationship and date Simon instead—this would still be a healthy approach to initiating a conversation that needs to happen.

The model described above is sometimes presented in therapeutic sessions in worksheet format. Practitioners of cognitive behavioral therapy will sometimes ask clients to complete "ABC" (antecedent, belief, consequence) worksheets, which typically look something like table 3 (examples from the perspective of "James" in the example described above). The ABC worksheet can be used to help improve one's relationship with all emotions, not just jealousy.

27. What are the warning signs of an abusive relationship?

Intimate partner violence can happen to anyone. A perpetrator of violence does not typically show obvious signs of being capable of that behavior early in the relationship. Sometimes, victims report drastic changes in their partner's behaviors after marriage or after parenthood. Meanwhile, by the time physical violence does occur, various other forms of control that were harder to see have already been gradually imposed upon the victim and entrenched to the point of feeling normal—such as lack of social supports and financial resources, gaslighting (denying what happened in a way that leads the victim to doubt their own perception of what is going on), and blame. By the time more obvious signs of physical aggression present themselves, leaving the relationship becomes fraught with complications.

For many, the term "abuse" connotes physical violence, but actually, abuse is more about control. An abuser uses various tactics (not limited to violence) to exert their will over another person as a way of compensating for their own unmet psychological needs. As was mentioned regarding sexual assault in question 20, it is important to examine ways to prevent abuse from a perpetrator's perspective, not just a victim's. The question "How can I avoid abusing someone?" is just as important as "How can I avoid becoming a victim of abuse?"

In the early 1980s, feminist Ellen Pence developed a model for a domestic violence prevention program in Duluth, Minnesota. The model captures the various layers through which abusers seek power and control. Though it has its critics, the Duluth Model, as it is now known, is the most influential framework for identifying and discussing abuse dynamics. These include:

- *Isolation*: Forbidding or preventing a partner from maintaining relationships with friends and family; pressuring them to give up or neglect those relationships; discouraging or preventing them from confiding in others about problems in the relationship; or controlling access to information, mental health services, or other outside influences.
- *Minimizing/blaming*: Gaslighting the partner by trying to make them believe acts of abuse didn't happen or were not that serious, blaming the partner for "making" the abuser act violently or aggressively, not taking the partner's concerns seriously.
- *Dependency*: Setting up systems in the relationship that make the partner dependent and thus less able to leave the relationship or stand up for themselves. The most common example of this is controlling finances or preventing the partner from getting their own employment, emotional support, or other resources.
- *Emotional manipulation*: Making critical or contemptuous comments, shaming, blaming, and gaslighting.
- *Use of privilege*: Defining gender roles—using traditional gender roles in a way that further subverts power and influence (for example, a male partner in a heterosexual relationship insisting on being the "head of the household" and having final say in major decisions).
- *Use of children*: Threatening to cut off access to children if there is any disloyalty, saying things designed to make the other person feel guilty about what could happen to the children if they don't stay in the relationship, using children to relay messages.

- *Violence and intimidation*: Out-of-control expressions of anger, breaking things, threatening violence, threatening suicide, displaying weapons, threatening legal actions, abusing pets.

A person who can trust a partner to not hurt or abandon them is less likely to resort to the above behaviors (see questions 23 and 25 for more about jealousy). On the other side of that coin, a person who is confident and practices assertive communication is at less risk of becoming the victim in an abusive relationship. However, it is important to stress that abuse can be perpetrated by anybody, and it can happen to anybody, largely because the systems that perpetuate it fall into place so gradually, and often unconsciously. In general, the following practices can help ward off abusive dynamics in a relationship:

- Own your emotions, and make space for them. Have a variety of tools and resources for coping with and overcoming difficult emotions, especially shame, anger, and fear.
- Avoid gaslighting. Respect the other person's reality. Instead of saying, "I never did that" or "That never happened," say, "I don't remember it that way" or "We had different experiences of that situation."
- Monitor feelings of isolation. Maintain social outlets outside your primary relationship. Encourage your partner to maintain outside relationships and to exercise their own judgment about which relationships are healthy for them. Confide in others about challenges in your relationship, and encourage your partner to do the same. Engage regularly and frequently with at least one or two pastimes that do not involve your partner.
- Be careful with substance use. Notice if you tend to use substances to escape negative feelings or if you use substances to excess. Abusive behaviors are more likely to be perpetrated and tolerated when alcohol or other drugs are involved.
- Take transgressions seriously. Any person may slip up and act or speak aggressively from time to time. It is meaningful to take that action seriously and demonstrate accountability through concrete steps to avoid repeating those actions. If a partner gives feedback about feeling hurt, listen. Seek counseling if needed (see question 40).
- Monitor feelings of depression or stuckness. Such feelings may or may not indicate abuse in your relationship, but they deserve attention and support regardless. Obsessions or frequent fantasizing about escape or rescue are warning signs. Access a variety of resources to address feeling trapped, hopeless, helpless, lonely, or desperate.

- Take responsibility for your own past. Even though the abuse or neglect you experienced in childhood or in other relationships was not your fault, only you can take the steps necessary for healing. Failure to do so puts you at more risk for perpetuating abuse or for tolerating future abuse.

28. Should I tolerate abuse or violence from my partner or threats of violence (even if toward themselves) if I know they are actually a good person underneath?

People commonly confuse themselves about whether a relationship is abusive by assessing the character of the person who may be exhibiting aggressive or controlling behaviors. Most humans prefer to believe that "good people" don't do bad things or that if they have done bad things, their better nature will motivate them to change. If our partner has a sympathetic backstory or engages in good works in other areas of their life, we are reluctant to believe they are capable of abusing us. Unfortunately, this is a fallacy. In fact, some abusers work hard to cultivate an image of a "good person," either by painting themselves as a victim of circumstances or by contributing to the community through volunteer work or other acts. This mindset applies to the self as well. If you believe yourself to be a "good person," you might never consider that you would unwittingly abuse someone important to you. Even "good people" can experience hard times that bring up personal demons that were previously unknown, possibly leading to patterns of fear and desperation that facilitate abusive actions. "Good people" may despise their own harmful actions or feel ashamed, but that does not mean they are motivated to change. The only true sign of motivation is action. (For more on distinguishing how to "accept" a partner's imperfections versus "settling" for less than you deserve, see question 38.)

Another way people confuse themselves is by excusing violent acts as "out of character." It can be tempting to say, "He has only hit me a couple of times when he was really angry" or "She only acts that way when she's drunk; otherwise, she's fine." According to the National Coalition Against Domestic Violence, controlling behaviors that are less obvious than physical or sexual assault are often operating in the background, drawing less attention and feeding confusion about the severity of the situation. "Although physical assaults may occur only occasionally, they instill fear of future violent attacks," which allows even more control to be exerted over the victim.

When abusive dynamics do become more obvious, the victim may excuse behaviors out of loyalty and a desire not to penalize their partner for their own abuse history, mental health problems, or difficulty handling stress. Often, perpetrators of violence feel guilt, shame, and disgust at their behavior, but, unfortunately, the presence of these feelings is often mistaken as motivation for change. In deciding whether to continue in a relationship with a person who is being abusive, it can be helpful to remember the distinction between forgiving a behavior and excusing that behavior. It is possible for you to choose a nonjudgmental or loving attitude toward a person who is lashing out aggressively without continuing to expose yourself to any behaviors that are not healthy for you to experience. An abuser's proven willingness to take meaningful and concrete steps toward change may provide hope that the relationship can be salvaged, but it is more often the case that the relationship must be sacrificed in order to provide both partners the space and impetus to engage in the personal work necessary to transform themselves.

In trying to support a person experiencing abuse, a well-meaning friend or family member may unwittingly engage in their own forms of controlling, coercive, or manipulative behavior. While none may seem like the obvious answer to the above question, in reality, each person has the right and responsibility to determine for themselves what their boundaries are and when and how to enforce them. It is one thing to advise zero tolerance for violence or threats, and it's quite another to face paying the costs associated with a zero tolerance policy. Sometimes those costs can be steep: loss of other relationships, less access to children, less financial or housing security, and risks of more violence are just a few of the common concerns a person must weigh when deciding if they will leave an abusive relationship. Only the person in that situation can determine when they are ready to pay those costs. If you would like to help an adult who is their own legal guardian and who you believe is experiencing abuse, respect their capacity to direct their own lives. Be honest about your concerns, but stop short of pressuring them in one direction or the other. Celebrate their strengths, and build their overall confidence. Offer your unconditional support, love, and willingness to listen. In many cases, having a trustworthy ear outside the relationship is enough on its own to give the person what they need to make the healthiest decision for themselves.

29. Can my relationship be healthy if one or both of us has an addiction or a mental health diagnosis?

Watching a loved one struggle with a mental illness or addiction can be excruciating. Not only are the behaviors that often come with these conditions often toxic for relationships, but also we miss out on being able to connect with the person we love. If our loved one seems to be drowning in panic, depression, obsession, or drugs, we may feel desperate to save them, partly because it's all we can think to do when a person is suffering and partly because we simply want to connect with the real person underneath. It can be hard to trust the other person to find their own way back to shore, but often, that is the only realistic choice.

According to the National Institute of Mental Health, about 20% of Americans live with an identified mental health problem. When you factor in the unknown millions who live with undiagnosed disorders related to anxiety, mood, or trauma, plus those who are coping with substance or behavioral addiction in all its various forms, it is no wonder that most relationships encounter challenges related to mental health. While it is not reasonable to expect two people who are unhealthy to have a healthy relationship, there are ways to work as a team and substantially mitigate the strain that mental health problems can put on relationships.

The most common hazard for relationships is failure to take individual responsibility for one's own mental health (see question 31 for more on codependency). This can fuel a dynamic in which partners are trying to compensate for each other's problems in ways that fuel toxic cycles. Consider the hypothetical couple Walter and Tim. Walter lives with diagnosed attention deficit hyperactivity disorder (ADHD) and undiagnosed PTSD from childhood abuse. The ADHD makes it difficult for him to stay organized and keep track of things, so Tim has taken on managing the finances and the schedule for the two of them and their two kids. Walter's PTSD makes him prone to aggressive outbursts when he feels criticized, so Tim is feeling more and more alone because he does not know how to discuss problems in their relationship without triggering a fight. Walter is increasingly less aware of his own weaknesses as Tim compensates for them. With Tim keeping everything organized, there are fewer consequences for Walter not managing his own ADHD. With Tim avoiding conflicts, there are fewer signs that would point to Walter needing treatment for PTSD.

Lest we imagine that Tim is innocent in this scenario, it is important to consider why he has chosen to take on all these burdens. In truth, Tim is living with undiagnosed anxiety. Like most people with unresolved anxiety, control strategies are a common coping method. Tim gets to feel more in control of his environment by managing the household. He holds power over Walter and is oblivious to the ways in which he enables Walter's increasing dependency on him, instead building more and more resentment about feeling alone at the top. Tim may feel as though he is benevolently supporting a wounded partner who does not appreciate him enough, but he is not aware of how self-serving this rescue project is. As power struggles and parent-child dynamics intensify, intimacy wanes. Increasingly lonely, Tim turns to alcohol with more frequency. As Tim builds resentments over Walter's weaknesses and perceived immaturity and Walter builds resentments over Tim's increasing emotional distance and substance abuse, they lose sight of each other's gifts and strengths. For example, Walter is an attentive and nurturing parent with a brilliant, creative mind, and Tim is a loyal and compassionate family man who fiercely stands up for his loved ones when they are being mistreated, but those qualities fade from awareness as mental health issues take center stage.

The antidote begins with establishing a culture of accountability and teamwork in the relationship. Walter and Tim must learn to sit in the driver's seat of their own personal growth, recognizing that they can request, but are not entitled to, assistance from their partner. This means marshaling support and resources from outside the relationship. For example, Walter decides to go to therapy for PTSD and starts listening to podcasts about developing organizational skills with ADHD. Tim talks to his doctor about medication for anxiety and starts attending Alcoholics Anonymous meetings. The two of them cheer each other on and celebrate the brave steps necessary to take new steps. As trust builds, they can start to discuss and heal the past from a place of humility (see question 37 on forgiveness). With even more healing and trust-building, they can start to challenge one another. Walter can say, "I feel like you're growing more distant," and Tim is much more likely to hear it without defensiveness compared to when betrayals were fresh and they were both stewing in resentments.

If you live with an addiction or a mental health diagnosis, your best bet for being capable of a healthy relationship is to create and maintain your own system of support, resources, and healthy practices for coping and healing that exists independent of a partner or potential partner. Then a partner can join or participate in this system if they choose, without feeling anxious that you will flounder without their heroic efforts.

30. Can a relationship help me overcome past abuse or trauma?

Popular culture romanticizes the idea of a romantic relationship healing a tragic figure. The classic fairy tale "Beauty and the Beast," popularized by Disney, is perhaps the most egregious of countless examples. No wonder so many people grow up thinking that they can "save" a wounded partner or that they can change an unhealthy person with the power of their love. Part of what gives the trope so much appeal is that there are grains of truth in it. A person who has done terrible things likely experienced terrible things that fed into that behavior, and they may still have honorable qualities that are worth nurturing. Such a person may carry shame about their past that requires healing, and having someone else learn about all their flaws and still offer acceptance and love is a powerful antidote for shame. But there are limits to that process—most notably, that it never works if only one person is responsible for delivering the acceptance and love to the tragic figure. The wounded person must be actively seeking healing from a variety of sources. A healthy intimate relationship can *help* heal trauma, but it is not the centerpiece of that process. All too often, well-meaning partners wind up suffering in abusive relationships when they imagined they had the power to save or heal a violent person (see question 30 on codependency).

What is familiar can feel safe, even if it isn't. If you grew up in a home with little or no boundaries, you are more likely to find relationships in adulthood that have little or no boundaries because that feels normal. You know how to navigate that. If you grew up with abuse, you may feel you don't deserve a partner who respects you. Part of your identity is connected to the experience of abuse, so you may feel too uncomfortable with a partner who treats you well. Conversely, making a conscious effort to break the pattern and seek partners who are healthy requires mustering the courage to wade into unfamiliar territory. You can't predict what will happen, and your old coping skills will be of little use. However, you will grow, and being treated better can gradually become the new normal.

In a 2021 article for *Psychology Today*, clinical psychologist Ingrid Clayton illuminated the neurobiology behind what is known as "trauma-bonding." She explained:

> When we are faced with abuse and neglect, we are chemically wired to focus on getting to the "other side." When the abuser is [also] the person that brings us relief, the brain associates them with safety.
>
> The brain latches on to the positive experience of relief rather than the negative impact of the abuser. . . . Trauma-bonding is a hormonal attachment created by repeated abuse, sprinkled with being "saved" every now and then. A slightly different version of this cycle can be seen when we are sitting at a slot machine in Vegas. It's called intermittent reinforcement, and casinos have long used the data surrounding it to help us pour our life savings into their hands in the hope that we might finally "win."

It can be tempting to think that a relationship has the power to heal you or your partner's trauma, but there is substantial risk of simply repeating the same pattern experienced with past abusers. When we ask a person to heal us, we hand them tremendous power, and they are likely not equipped to handle it well.

Of course, arriving at the willingness to choose a different type of relationship requires a certain amount of healing in advance. Here we find a chicken-and-egg question: "Do I get healthier because my relationships got healthier, or did my relationships get healthier because I got healthier?" The real answer, of course, is that they happen in tandem, pulling each other along, like two heavy balls joined by an elastic band. Improving your relationship with yourself is the best catalyst; that way, you're not waiting for someone to come along and "rescue" you. It can also help to keep the "s" in "relationships." One relationship, no matter how healthy, has less potential to help you along a healing path than a variety of healthy connections with friends, support groups, coworkers, professional helpers, and so on.

31. How can I tell if I am codependent or in a codependent relationship?

The term "codependent" originally described a person addicted to an addict. For example, an alcoholic suffers from a physical or emotional dependency on alcohol; the codependent suffers from an emotional dependency on the relationship with the alcoholic. Over the years, the term "codependent" has evolved to describe anyone who prioritizes accommodating a needy person (such as an addict, a narcissist, or anyone else who can't or won't take responsibility for their own needs) at the expense of their own wellness. In her groundbreaking 1987 book *Codependent No More*, Melody Beattie characterized codependence as a compulsion to rescue or enable others or "to feel responsible for other people's feelings, thoughts, actions, choices, wants, needs, well-being, lack of well-being and ultimate destiny." She describes how codependents can become "lost in someone else's problem" and "forget how to take care of [themselves]."

Feminist scholar Alison Favorini called it "the search for self-identity through external relationships." Considering the essential role of identity in psychological health and safety, Favorini's definition points to the visceral psychological hunger for attachment that codependents experience. Perhaps the most influential definition of "identity" came from German psychologist Erik Erikson, who explained that identity continuously develops throughout the life span as a result of various influences, including experiences, values, beliefs, memories, and relationships. Notice that "relationships" is only one of the factors that contribute to identity and that it is plural. Unhealthy relationships often begin when two people who don't love themselves try to love each other. Many people who grew up in dysfunctional families believe they need to find their "true love" to feel complete. If your "true love" has an addiction or some other limitation and is not taking adequate responsibility for it, your own sense of safety becomes wrapped up in taking care of them.

If one or more of your primary caregivers in your childhood did not or could not maintain emotional stability, you are at particularly high risk for codependency. A child's sense of their own safety depends on the stability and trustworthiness of their caregivers. Imagine being taken hostage and learning that you could prevent your otherwise insane captor from harming you if you kept them comfortable—empathize, tell jokes, bring them snacks, and avoid making trouble or having any imperfections or needs of your own. If that situation carried on for years, keeping yourself safe by making others comfortable would become your primary way of relating to people. A relationship with someone who is already comfortable and therefore does not require those services would feel unnatural. You would instead gravitate to those who are emotionally immature, unstable, or compromised in some way.

Codependents are drawn to people with tragic backstories or other forms of vulnerability or weakness. They often believe they are very giving, sacrificing, and nurturing people. While these can, of course, be admirable qualities, in excess, they become problematic. A codependent may be using caretaking as a way to compensate for, or avoid, their own unresolved trauma or anxiety. In this way, their relentless giving becomes invisibly self-serving. Overly accommodating another person leads that person to increased dependency on the caretaking figure, which gives that caretaker a greater sense of power over the other person (the last thing a codependent wants is for their partner to be independent and self-reliant; the codependent would then feel less needed and less in control). Codependents often impose unauthorized transactions on relationships—unstated bargains like "If I sacrifice for you, then you'll love me more." Often, resentments develop, as the person providing care continues to feel underappreciated and lonely, but their partner never signed off on this invisible contract. Codependents struggle to maintain integrity and keep healthy boundaries (see question 25). They may be overly loyal, staying in abusive or unsatisfying situations for too long because they are relying on the relationship to provide identity or to numb the pain of a lonely or chaotic childhood. They may feel guilty or selfish if they are not actively caretaking or sacrificing for someone else—a reaction conditioned into them by a past abuser as a way of ensuring that the abuser's needs remain the focus of attention.

It is possible for codependence to manifest in other types of relationships, not just intimate partnerships. Sometimes people are codependent with their children, sibling(s), a friend, or even a boss or toxic workplace. There are many ways to narrow one's experiences of intimacy, meaning, identity, and love down to an external person or environment. In any situation, codependency can be just as toxic as narcissism or addiction. Healthy relationships are built on trust, and it is difficult to trust a person who lacks integrity and is not getting their needs met.

Thinking of codependency as an addiction can provide a helpful framework for self-assessment. When assessing if someone is addicted to a substance, one common test is to determine how well the person functions without access to that substance. If you think of a relationship as your sole or primary source of happiness or if you find yourself obsessively preoccupied with the idea of finding a relationship, you may be codependent. If your identity is mostly defined by a connection to someone else, to the point where you don't develop independent interests, friendships, or goals, you may be codependent.

Codependence is not the same as "interdependence," which describes two equal partners trusting each other with tasks and responsibilities with explicit and healthy communication and a culture of teamwork and mutual accountability. A couple may rely on each other for a variety of forms of assistance, from meal preparation to emotional support or even long-term care during an injury or illness, but as long as each partner knowingly and explicitly agrees to the arrangement, feels fed and treated fairly in the relationship, and has a variety of other resources also sustaining their wellness, the arrangement can be rewarding and sustainable.

Psychotherapy can be helpful in correcting the habits of codependency. Co-Dependents Anonymous (CoDA) meetings offer free support, fellowship, and guidance on a 12-step program for recovery from the unhealthy patterns learned in childhood, which Beattie describes as a lifelong project. In recovery, codependents learn to develop healthier and more diverse sources of identity, protect their own integrity, and trust that love and purpose are abundant and come in many different forms. In many cases, the simple act of devoting more of your resources (time, money) into your own care is a powerful start all by itself. Sometimes, recovery from codependency is as simple as directing to oneself an equal amount of the nurturing, attention, and service that had been amply given to others.

Healthy Conflict

32. Is conflict a sign of an unhealthy relationship?

It can be tempting to view harmony as the ultimate goal of a relationship, but the healthiest relationships feature mutual growth as well as harmony. Growth comes from challenging one another. Harmony is preserved by handling differing opinions and competing values with respect and patience, not by denying or avoiding conflict.

Basketball legend Charles Barkley explained during a recent NBA broadcast how two veteran players helped him turn his career around when he was a rookie. Barkley approached them and asked why he wasn't getting more playing time, and they told him, "You are too fat and too slow." Barkley explained that he felt hurt by this feedback at first but eventually took it as constructive criticism, worked on his body, and blossomed into a Hall of Fame player.

This story beautifully illustrates the power of trust in helping individuals meet their true potential in a relationship. The reason Barkley was able to convert the criticism into motivation was that he trusted that his teammates wanted what was best for him—they weren't simply taking out their own frustrations on him by being mean. Their blunt message also communicated a secondary truth: "We know it is more important to you to become a better player than to have your feelings protected." This undoubtedly speaks to some experiences of healthy team bonding that took place before the conversation in question, some trust-building that helped establish a certain level of emotional safety. It also helped that Barkley sought their input; their comments may not have landed as well had they been unsolicited.

When couples enter relationship therapy, there is often much criticism happening, very little of it with invitation (see question 14 for more about how criticism hampers connection and trust). Unsolicited criticism is one of many forms of aggression that are toxic for relationships. Here, we uncover an important distinction: conflict is healthy and normal; aggression is unhealthy and must be eradicated. Couples must learn to stop pointing fingers and instead work together to build a culture of teamwork, where they each learn to trust that even when they disagree, they are still on the same team and want what's best for each other. This requires building grounding skills, soothing fears, embracing accountability, and opening channels of empathy so that the selfish power-grabs that come with a sense of feeling threatened can dissipate (see question 15 on trust-building).

Every successful team, and every meaningful relationship, experiences conflict. Trust and loyalty are sustained by skilled conflict resolution, including negotiation, compromise, humility, and acceptance of limitations. With these qualities present, everyone involved can grow as a result of challenging one another. Often, when a couple does not argue or fight much, one or both of the people in that relationship have chosen to "avoid" conflict by not discussing problems or trying to solve them alone, perhaps by giving in to whatever the other person wants. This strategy does not eliminate conflict, it merely houses it within the person, where it is more likely to feed resentment and impede genuine connection. Some people so closely associate the idea of conflict with aggression and harm that they deny that the conflict exists or minimize problems in order to try to feel safe. Relationships can carry on for years this way, with a relatively low quality of intimacy and connection. Aggression may be mostly out of the picture, but one could argue that settling for a long-term relationship with chasms of distance from unresolved conflicts is just as, if not more, harmful.

33. How can my partner and I improve our communication?

Often, when couples say they are struggling with communication, they think they need to improve how they say things so their partner will understand better. While it can be helpful to package one's message in artful diction that lands gently on the other person's ears, this is only a fraction of the work. The most important aspect of communication is willingness to listen and to develop listening skills, which includes absorbing the important truths in a message that may not have been delivered with pristine tact.

Borrowing one more basketball example: in the ESPN/Netflix documentary series "The Last Dance," which chronicled the culture and interpersonal dynamics of the dominant 1990s-era Chicago Bulls, Michael Jordan addressed criticism of his intensely harsh and demanding leadership style, by saying, "I never asked anyone to do anything that I wouldn't do." Nothing undermines leadership like hypocrisy, but Jordan knew that he had to hold himself to the highest standard if he wanted his teammates to listen to him at all. Struggling couples would do well to consider this example. Rather than focusing exclusively on what you are not getting from your partner, assess your own willingness to provide that very same thing. Usually the "thing" in question is listening, preferably with some genuine openness and willingness to empathize.

Listening is always an option and never a bad idea. Even if your partner is closed off, choosing not to speak, listening is still possible. The very act of not speaking says, "I don't feel safe to share what is going on inside me." Think about what that must be like. Your nonverbal partner may also be speaking through body language, turning away from you, avoiding eye contact, or making frustrated gestures. You can demonstrate listening by reflecting what you see: "It looks like you are feeling upset and don't want to have this conversation right now. I can respect that." On the other hand, if your partner is expressing anger or even rage, skilled listening is an effective intervention. The only time that listening is not necessarily the best idea is when the need to maintain a boundary or maintain personal safety takes precedence.

In many situations, setting aside your desire to express yourself so that you can focus on listening feels like a sacrifice. The idea of serving the needs of a person you feel has hurt you feels like an injustice. This attitude must be corrected if you are truly committed to improving communication. In reality, listening is an act of service for the relationship itself, not just for the other person. Listening also brings direct benefits to the listener. Consider that unless you are a child or otherwise dependent on someone for survival, relationships are a choice. A person who has hurt your feelings is also a person with whom you choose to maintain a connection, presumably because you respect them and feel they enrich your life. That enrichment will not always take a comfortable form. Seeking greater understanding of how they feel and why they are feeling it, even when their form of expression is uncomfortable, invites an expansion of your awareness and connectivity as you explore new territories of intimacy with someone you value. If the relationship is generally healthy, you can trust that the other person will also be willing to listen to you in due time.

The internet offers boundless resources on active listening skills. Typically, it helps to practice genuine curiosity with the speaker. This does not necessarily mean interrupting them with questions. It can mean paying attention not just to the content or information being shared, but also to other layers of the speaker's experience, such as what they intend or hope will happen as a result of sharing and what emotion they are experiencing as they share. Asking questions that invite the speaker to reveal more about their experience (as opposed to leading or argumentative questions) can be helpful on a limited basis. Commonly, communication experts also recommend eye contact, open posture, and nonverbal acknowledgments (such as nodding) as important active listening skills. Reflecting a summary of what you've heard is an effective way to build trust, by letting the speaker know that you were paying attention and have absorbed their message.

When it comes to speaking, the most tried and true rule is to stick with "I statements," which means talking about your own feelings and experiences rather than accusing or labeling the other person's behavior. "You're not picking up after yourself enough around here" becomes "I feel overwhelmed at the mess and clutter, and I feel alone in trying to correct it. Can we work on a solution?" As mentioned in question 11 earlier, a "no complaining" rule can help you keep the culture of your relationship positive. "No complaining" doesn't mean problems are not addressed, but they are addressed with a sense of opportunity, celebrating potential for improvement rather than picking apart what's wrong. For example, "I'm tired of having the same three meals all the time" becomes "How about if we put our heads together and think of some fun new dinner ideas?" Which would you rather hear from a partner or family member?

Sometimes, communication is not the real problem. "We have a healthy relationship, we just need to learn how to communicate better" is a common refrain among those starting couples therapy. A relationship may feel "healthy" (i.e., normal) to its participants, but exploring the communication patterns sometimes reveals underlying barriers that impair openness, such as patterns of abuse or neglect, poor self-care and inattention to mental health, or feelings of insecurity related to power imbalances. Problematic relationship dynamics can be difficult to fully comprehend from within the relationship. A professional relationship counselor can help determine if your challenges can be overcome merely by building communication skills or if there are other dynamics that need to be addressed.

34. What are the best ways to make decisions or resolve conflicts as a couple?

Resolving conflict effectively requires taking personal responsibility for the things that drive us to claim power over another person. Fear is the most common of these. Once fears are named, opportunities emerge to identify common hopes and goals and to approach the conflict like a puzzle that requires creative ingenuity to solve.

Some people take a transformative approach to disagreements, and others tend to take a transactional approach. It can help to be mindful about which you are using and why. A transformative approach seeks to change someone's opinion or feelings. If you tend to try to persuade someone to see things your way or do what you want or if you are hoping they will empathize or sympathize with your perspective, you are probably using a transformative approach. This tends to work best when everyone involved in the dispute is open minded and willing to consider other points of view or new facts or when a third party is available to facilitate a sense of safety. Transformative strategies include not only argument, but also sharing of feelings or experiences, attempting to increase empathy and understanding through mutual vulnerability. Increasing empathy and understanding undermine the fear that is usually the culprit of entrenched conflicts. With fear reduced and empathy increased, the brain is more capable of creative problem-solving. Some people prefer a transformative approach because they believe they can change others but are not actually willing to allow another person's argument or perspective to influence their own thinking. Don't be like that.

A transactional approach is often overlooked but is, in many cases, more efficient and more effective. Transactional conflict resolution eschews any effort to change either side's position or feelings and instead focuses on negotiation and creative problem-solving. Working in more concrete terms makes it easier to respect each person's voice and integrity. Couples who are good at managing conflict have an array of transactional strategies at their disposal. They do not always feel the need to fully see one another's reality in order to make progress.

Consider the example of the fictional couple Dave and Ingrid. They met through a dating app and live a couple of hours away from each other, but after about 18 months of messaging, video calls, and weekend visits, they feel ready to move in together. Both have jobs near where they live, so both would prefer not to relocate. Both carry some fear into the conversation. Ingrid remembers losing her own sense of identity when she moved into an ex-boyfriend's place several years ago. She knows that choosing a space and making it her own is an important tool for her to feel she has freedom and autonomy. Dave fears the inevitable conflicts that arise when people cohabitate—bickering about dirty dishes, expenses, and so forth reminds him of the months leading up to his parents' divorce when he was 12 years old. Generally, he prefers to avoid conflict. After some work to understand, validate, and give care to each other's feelings, as well as some unproductive discussions in which they tried to convince each other that their fears are irrational, they set aside transformative approaches and decide to try negotiation and compromise.

The first thing for Dave and Ingrid to decide is where to live. The obvious compromise here would be for Dave and Ingrid to find a new apartment about halfway between their current residences and split all the responsibilities and expenses 50/50. Unfortunately, life is rarely that simple. The area between their two cities is rural, and both much prefer an urban lifestyle.

Ingrid shares her concern about moving into another person's space and losing her identity. Dave immediately offers to move to Ingrid's place and take on the long commute to his job. He feels more comfortable self-sacrificing than risking Ingrid feeling any type of burden, which could lead to conflict. Fortunately, Dave had already discussed his fear of conflict and promised to work on it and take feedback about it. Ingrid spots his old avoidance tactic immediately and challenges him to think about what he would be giving up and whether he would truly be at peace with this sacrifice. After some reflection, Dave realizes that gas is expensive and he might eventually start feeling stress and resentment about the commute. He rejoins the conversation with an offer to move to Ingrid's place and have her pay a slightly higher share of the bills and housework so that there is more room in his budget for gas and more time in his schedule for the long drives. Ingrid is tempted to immediately accept this proposal; having more responsibility over the space (particularly because it was hers first) seems to give her the extra authority over it that would assuage her fears. However, Ingrid remembers something her therapist said recently: unless you live alone, control over a space is pretty closely tied to control over other people. Ingrid had already made a commitment to herself and to Dave to work on being less controlling and more trusting. She counterproposes to find another apartment in her city that they can pick out together. Dave agrees.

Notice that Dave and Ingrid are not just discussing where to live and how to divide responsibilities. Under the surface, they are also determining the decision-making culture in their relationship. It can be helpful to make that part of the conversation explicit. Some decisions need to be made with equal authority, which means hammering out compromise. Compromise means each person acknowledges they won't get everything they want, but if they give something up, it's because they are getting something else. For example, Ingrid prefers a living space with lots of windows and light, but those apartments tend to be more expensive, and Dave has a limited budget. She may have to give that up in exchange for Dave agreeing to a place that is pet-friendly. Compromise works best when neither party carries resentments about what they gave up because they value the process more than the result.

Some decisions can be made by one person because the other person has no interest or preference. For example, the couple knows that Ingrid is not very picky about food and is not interested in cooking, so they decide that Dave can have all the authority about groceries and meals. This format of decision-making works best when the person giving up authority truly and authentically does not care about the issue so that there are no resentments or critiques coming down the line (you'll never hear Ingrid complain about Dave's meat loaf). It also works best when there are other areas in which the authority is reversed—for example, Dave could not care less about what kind of neighborhood they live in. He gladly cedes 100% authority to Ingrid because he has better things to think about. This comes with the understanding that he won't be making grumpy comments later about how the houses are too close together around here, there aren't enough coffee shops nearby, and so on.

Certain types of decisions are best made with a "majority rule/minority rights" principle: one person takes on the final authority in the decision, with the promise to fully hear and consider the other person's needs and wishes in that decision. For example, because Ingrid has stronger skills and preferences about interior decorating, she takes on more authority in that area. Dave has little interest in thinking about furniture or art on the walls, but he is grateful that Ingrid checked with him because he does feel somewhat stressed by his tight budget. Ingrid agrees to make all the decisions about interior decorating and to keep the spending within a certain limit. This format of decision-making builds trust from both sides: Dave is trusting Ingrid to follow through with her promise to be careful about spending, and Ingrid is trusting Dave to be content with her decisions and not come back with criticism later. Again, this format also works best if there are other areas in which the roles are reversed.

Of course, as hard as any couple might work to anticipate and plan for effective conflict resolution, many surprise situations will emerge, and decisions will not always be made with perfect respect for everyone's

power and interests. The good news is that willingness to revisit and discuss the decisions and to tend to the overall culture of mutual respect and
equality creates a solid foundation that can help a relationship weather
any temporary setbacks or hurt feelings.

35. How can my partner and I deal with anger in a healthy way?

Hockey players have a particular method of dealing with anger and conflict: fighting. It's their way of expressing displeasure and holding each
other accountable. And there are rules around it. First and foremost, anyone who steps onto the ice has a clear understanding that fighting is part
of the game. No one is going to be surprised if they are challenged to combat after breaking rules that the officials either don't see or can't enforce.
Players get fair warning, so they can adequately defend themselves; no
one gets sucker punched. Gloves are removed before fighting, and only
a few types of strikes are allowed, mainly punches to the head area, and
maybe occasionally, the torso or abdomen. Players generally fight other
players their own size. No one fights against goaltenders, probably because
goaltenders wear extra equipment and are therefore at a disadvantage (on
rare occasions when goalies do fight, they fight each other). Generally,
referees will allow players to fight until someone gains a clear advantage
and there is a greater risk of injury, such as when one of the combatants
falls to the ice. None of these fighting rules are in the official rule book;
players just know and accept them as part of hockey culture.

Crucially, players must understand that the same rules for expressing
anger and resolving conflict do not apply when they leave the ice and
return to their personal lives. They don't expect non-hockey players to
understand the rules of conflict resolution in hockey culture. That would
be ridiculous. Yet people enter relationships and new environments all
the time expecting others to know and play by the same rules of conflict
that they grew up with. A person's way of dealing with conflict and anger
is mostly informed by the family and culture in which they were raised.
When we reach adulthood, we are sometimes challenged to adapt to new
cultural norms of dealing with conflict, such as when we partner with
someone who is used to different methods of conflict resolution (or non-
resolution). Think about the ways in which conflict was handled in your
community or family growing up. Does the culture you come from differ
from the culture in which you want to assimilate? Does your partner know
your native culture's rules of expressing anger?

The 2005 book *A Framework for Understanding Poverty*, by Ruby Payne, PhD, offers groundbreaking insights about the intersection between social class and culture and the implications for institutions like schools and courts, which purport to serve everyone equally. Payne points out that cultural norms differ not only based on ethnicity and geography but also on social class. In fact, patterns emerge about class culture that are consistent even when other aspects of culture like ethnicity or religion are different.

According to Payne, the culture of economic class influences the ways in which we relate to one another on numerous levels. For example, in generational poverty, a person's identity is closely tied to their relationships, so preservation of those relationships tends to take priority over other considerations, such as individual achievement. In middle-class culture, identity is built more around achievements, while those steeped in wealth culture are more likely to develop identity around legacy, pedigree, or possessions. Decision-making differs as well. In generational poverty, decisions are based on a sense of day-to-day survival and short-term sources of entertainment, while the middle class makes decisions based on work and achievement, and wealthy people tend to prioritize building or maintaining social, financial, or political connections. Perhaps the most striking illustration of the cultural differences between these classes, as described in Payne's model, is conflict resolution. The wealthy resolve conflicts through lawyers or through social inclusion or exclusion, while those in the middle-class value resolving conflict with words or by accessing institutions designed to serve them (i.e., calling the police). Payne points out that those in generational poverty usually lack access to such tools or are less likely to believe they will work for them and instead use physical fighting or threats of violence to address conflicts.

Payne is careful not to imply that any class culture is superior or inferior to any other (indeed, any of the paradigms summarized above can lead to traumatic experiences) but encourages increased awareness of when a person from a background of poverty is being asked to assimilate to an institution that operates with middle-class values, such as public school. This book itself offers recommendations based largely on middle-class values. The section on codependence, for example, discourages overreliance on external relationships as a source of identity. This book recommends against aggression, even though people who have chronic experiences of their survival being in question have likely found aggression to be pretty useful in maintaining social order and getting needs met. The very fact that it is a book, written by a person with government-issued credentials (a mental health counseling license), invites trust in institutions, though people who live in poverty are reluctant to trust institutions because institutions don't tend to serve their interests very well, and people who are used to wealth don't trust institutions because they are too easily manipulated. Do you and your partner come from similar cultural backgrounds? Did your partner come from a family or community where it was common for people to yell and scream at each other and then all was forgotten, whereas you come from a background in which people did not express their anger at all? Mindfully and mutually designing a culture and set of rules for conflict resolution and anger management with your partner can be a helpful step.

Thankfully, there are some facts of human psychology that remain consistent across cultures. Perhaps the most useful and transcendent guide ever written about how to deal with anger is *The Autobiography of Martin Luther King, Jr.* In this collection of speeches, letters, essays, and journal entries, Dr. King recounts his experiences observing the way he and other African Americans were treated under segregation and other government-sanctioned racist practices in the mid-twentieth century; the seething rage that came with those experiences; and the leadership that inspired thousands to join a powerful movement for change without allowing anger to fuel hatred, violence, and dehumanization.

Anger is a natural emotion that is healthy to feel when we believe we have been treated unfairly. Feeling we have been treated unfairly is largely a function of our expectations. It can be helpful to examine expectations to assess if they are fair or realistic, including whether or not they come from a family or cultural background that does not match the current environment.

If we believe our expectations are fair and realistic, healthy processing of anger involves the pursuit of justice. Justice has two elements: (1) accountability, most often, the form of the witnessing and acknowledgment of the wrongdoing, ideally by the perpetrator(s), but also by society (this process is illustrated most clearly in the criminal justice system, where victims and their families hope to experience a form of validation and closure that comes with the system affirming their pain and attempting to address it by holding perpetrators accountable); and (2) healing, which requires everyone involved to regain their humanity and limit the degree to which they are burdened by pain and resentment over what happened. As Dr. King described it, giving in to violent urges only furthers the hatred and dehumanization that was at the root of the racist policies of the White establishment. To become scary only validated the racist establishment's fear- and hate-based view of people with darker skin. To most effectively seek justice, participants in the civil rights movement had to speak out and act in ways that preserved their integrity and their humanity. They put their lives on the line without sinking to the level of their violent oppressors.

Following this example in the context of a one-on-one relationship, we must first accept that injustice and anger will be part of the picture. Because people are not perfect, we will treat each other unfairly from time to time. Just as the criminal justice system operates most effectively when it is trustworthy and equally responsive to people from all backgrounds, your relationship needs a trustworthy method of handling conflict in order to make it easier for anger to be channeled in a positive direction (see questions 15 and 33). Practicing assertive communication skills can be a big help. In situations of conflict, some people engage in aggressive behavior or communication, which is defined as any behavior or communication that prioritizes one's own rights and needs above the other person's (for example, calling a friend a cruel name prioritizes your need to be heard about your anger over their need to be treated with dignity and respect). Other folks opt for passive behavior or communication, which is defined as prioritizing the other person's rights or needs above your own (neglecting your need to be heard in favor of the other person's perceived need to not experience too much stress, for example). Passive individuals fail to take responsibility for their anger and are at risk of allowing anger to build up over time, which can lead to sudden explosions of aggression even at seemingly small events (the proverbial "straw that broke the camel's back") or to learned helplessness and depression. People who behave and communicate assertively place everyone's rights and needs on equal footing. If you find that you've slipped into an aggressive or passive pattern, it can be helpful to take accountability for this and make a plan for being more assertive in the future (see question 36 for more about accountability).

Finding healthy and socially sanctioned ways to express anger can make a big difference. Anger is held in the body, so a person carrying anger often needs a response that honors the body's need for action and empowerment. This is why vigorous, power-based exercises (such as lifting weights or competitive sports) are such effective ways to channel anger. If athletic pursuits are not your style, it can be helpful to scream into a pillow, yell obscenities when alone in a car, or destroy objects that have no value, all of which give the body a sense of empowerment without harming anyone else. Expressing anger in creative pursuits such as art or music can also meet this need. These strategies don't necessarily foster the change needed for justice to be done, but they can help the person carrying anger avoid making things worse by having no outlets for that emotion.

Some psychologists describe anger as a "secondary emotion," meaning that it is fueled by another experience—namely, pain and fear. Mixing pain with some beliefs about why we are in pain or some fears about more pain that could happen in the future can fuel anger. Often, we carry pain and fear from events in our past, making us more sensitive and reactive to things that might happen in a current relationship. Correcting a pattern of anger in a way that is more sustainable than screaming into pillows every day involves enlisting some trustworthy help to open up about the pain and fear. For many people, anger feels like a much safer emotion to express than the more vulnerable fears or wounds that lie underneath. However, leaving those underlying emotions in the dark only empowers them to fester and increase potential harm. If you are in an intimate partnership and you feel angry more than occasionally, you owe it to yourself and your partner to find a safe and supportive environment in which you can begin to express and heal all the layers of your experience.

36. How can I offer a meaningful apology when I have hurt my partner?

The word "sorry" has several layers of meaning that can be confusing if the context is not clear. Sometimes it is used to express sympathy rather than contrition. Other times it is used as a way to try to diffuse anger or get out of "trouble," as if a parent is telling us, "Say you're sorry," after fighting with a sibling, and then all is forgotten. In order to relate authentically to self and others, it is important to be mindful when apologizing and only apologize when you truly feel you have mistreated someone and have acted in a way that conflicts with your values.

The most effective apologies come when there is no expected response from the other person. Do not apologize as a way to be forgiven or to restore connection. Do not apologize as a way of inviting the other person to apologize for their own wrongs. The best reason to apologize is to make things right with your own conscience—you know you have done something wrong, and you believe in owning it, helping the other person to heal, and avoiding that behavior in the future. Defending the actions or offering context may be valid and important tasks at some point, but not during an apology. Asking for accountability from someone else is also valid, but doing so during your own apology simply muddies the waters.

Offering a meaningful and accountable apology involves three steps:

1. Say the words "I'm sorry for . . . " or "I apologize for . . . " followed by a direct, specific, and non-sugarcoated, no euphemism description of the behavior. For example, saying "I'm sorry I got upset and acted badly, but I've just been super stressed out lately, and I felt hurt when you were ignoring me all morning" is not recommended. The words "got upset" and "acted badly" are too vague, and there is no place for explaining your own pain or the other person's bad behavior as part of an apology. Saying "I'm sorry for screaming obscenities at you and throwing your tablet in the river" is much better. It offers an unflinching description of the behavior without trying to soften the shame of it with further explanations or context.

2. Express empathy. Make an honest effort to acknowledge the other person's experience of your behavior. For example: "I imagine that when I lose control of my emotions it feels pretty scary for you, because you don't know what I might do or if you'll be safe. And having your tablet thrown in the river means that you now need to replace it, which is a whole extra task you didn't need right now." Even if you do not accurately capture what the other person's experience was, showing interest and willingness to understand goes a long way toward helping in their healing.

3. State your plan for correcting the impact of your behavior (if possible) and for not repeating the action, along with a willingness to be held accountable. For example: "I know that I get impulsive and vengeful when I feel angry. I've decided to check out a book from the library on anger management. If that doesn't seem to help, I'll sign up for counseling. If you'd like, I'll update you on my progress. Also, I will pay to replace your tablet." If you are struggling to come up with a plan for changing your behavior, then this step can become "I don't know how to stop myself from doing this in the future, but I'm open to suggestions. I'll also schedule an appointment with a therapist to see what they would recommend."

Apologizing is no one's idea of a good time, but if done well, it can serve as a springboard for healing, connection, and personal growth.

37. What is forgiveness, and when is it appropriate?

As mentioned in question 35, one aspect of justice is people being held accountable for harming others, but just as important is the task of healing for those who were victimized. Like it or not, those on the receiving end of harm done by others are still responsible for their own healing, which includes letting go of bitterness, resentment, or anger so that there is more room for happiness. It has often been said that "holding onto anger is like drinking poison and expecting the other person to die." Forgiving a person who has harmed you actually has very little to do with that person and everything to do with your relationship with yourself.

There are two common mistakes people make regarding forgiveness: (1) they try to forgive too soon, before other healing work has been done, and (2) they confuse forgiveness with trust. The late archbishop Desmond Tutu, author of *The Book of Forgiving*, points out that avoiding forgiveness because the other person doesn't "deserve" it or has not earned it only perpetuates victimization because it places the responsibility for your healing in the other person's hands. He writes, "If you can find it in yourself to forgive, you are no longer chained to the perpetrator." Often a person refusing to consider forgiveness is afraid that by letting go of the pain, they will not remain vigilant against being hurt again or is afraid of feeling like a doormat. Sometimes people want to stay angry to punish the other person, which accomplishes little except for the perpetuation of toxic imbalances of power. It can be helpful to remember that the decision to forgive and the decision to trust are two separate things. You might forgive your friend for forgetting to pick you up from the airport, but that doesn't mean you'll automatically trust that friend with the same task again in the future. You can take the additional step of asking yourself how your friend might earn back your trust, if you even want to give them that chance. There is no need to "punish" your friend or to protect yourself with hard feelings if you embrace the task of deciding and communicating what it would take for trust to be earned back or to accept that the other person has limitations (i.e., forgetfulness) that make them untrustworthy with certain tasks.

Just as problematic as holding onto resentment is the act of "forgiving too soon," which usually involves lying to oneself about readiness to let go of resentment and anger. In such situations, what is labeled forgiveness (i.e., acceptance of what can't be changed) is actually more of an attempt to sweep the past under the rug and forget about it. As you might expect, this does not solve anything. Truly letting go of the past involves work, rather than just saying you're doing it. Consider these steps:

- Name and acknowledge the facts of what you experienced.
- Allow yourself to feel the anger as well as the pain underneath. Reduce numbing or avoidance behaviors, like drugs or screen time. Experience and accept the pain.

- Express both the anger and the pain. Tell the story of what happened to you to anyone you trust to listen. Be creative. If possible, channel anger into something productive, such as advocating to prevent others (or yourself, if possible) experiencing the same injustice.
- Consciously release the pain with self-affirmations like "I'm letting that go" and "I don't need that anymore." It may sound hokey, but it works. Accept that it will take a while.
- Remember that anyone who has harmed you is not entitled to your trust until they have earned it. Decide what it will take for them to prove their worthiness, and communicate that.
- Consider ways in which you are also imperfect or have contributed to mutual problems. Reflect on whether you believe you are inherently better than anyone else or inherently incapable of harming others as badly as you've been harmed.

The play *The Crucible*, by Arthur Miller, offers a moving interpretation of forgiveness. It focuses on the Salem Witch Trials of 1692. But the major side plot revolves around the fact that the protagonist, John Proctor, had been unfaithful to his wife, Elizabeth, with the girl who started the witchcraft allegations. The marriage shows strain well into Act II. Proctor, despite showing signs of a guilty conscience, criticizes his wife's mistrust and resentment: "I have gone tiptoe in this house these last seven months. I have not moved from there to there without I think to please you, and still an everlasting funeral marches round your heart."

Elizabeth insists that she is not judging him. "I never thought you but a good man, John," she says, "only somewhat bewildered." As is often the case in struggling relationships, both are right. Elizabeth may be letting go of judgment, but her husband's efforts are not doing the trick to help her heal. He appears motivated to regain her trust and affection, but there is no clear way to accomplish this.

By the end of the play, when Proctor is deciding if he will confess to witchcraft or be executed, he asks Elizabeth to forgive him. She answers, "It come to naught that I should forgive you, if you'll not forgive yourself." Having reflected on her own record, she confesses to her husband, "I have my own sins to count. It needs a cold wife to prompt lechery." Proctor interprets this as Elizabeth taking responsibility for his choices, but that's not what she's going for. She simply finds more utility in confronting her own shortcomings. She confesses that her own insecurities prevented her from loving her husband warmly. She recognizes that her husband is responsible for his infidelity, but they are both responsible for creating a relationship culture that is healthy or unhealthy. Did Elizabeth's limitations contribute indirectly to John's decision to have an affair? That's debatable, but the debate has little value. Better to see if both are willing to take responsibility for being better people and better partners.

The Book of Forgiving offers this quote, attributed to actor Lily Tomlin: "Forgiveness means giving up hope for a better past." No one has ever more aptly and succinctly expressed the absurdity of holding on to anger rather than using it and letting it go. At the same time, the decision to forgive is a very personal one. If you have been harmed, no other person has the right to dictate when and how you might forgive. That choice is yours alone. Assess for yourself whether you have done the other healing work required to authentically move on from the past.

38. How do I know if I'm "accepting" my partner versus "settling" for less than I deserve?

What people are willing to put up with varies by context. Harvard University psychologist Daniel Gilbert uses this analogy during one of his TED talks on happiness: "If you go out on a first date with a guy and he picks his nose, you probably won't go on a second date with him. But if you're married to a guy for 25 years and he picks his nose, you say, 'Well, he has a heart of gold; don't touch the fruitcake.'"

One simple way to differentiate "accepting" from "settling" is to remember that it is healthy to *accept* what we can't change, including the past and the present as it is constituted in this moment. There is no such thing as "accepting" a future. It is possible (arguably necessary) to accept the past and present while pursuing change. To accept something does not necessitate giving up on goals and ambitions, it only helps to make our expectations more reasonable. To "accept" is to make peace with the past and the present, to stop fighting with reality. To "settle" is to fail to strive for a better future.

Understanding the difference between "accepting" and "settling" requires rigorous honesty with self about what constitutes an infringement on integrity and wellness as opposed to what can be chalked up to an annoyance we can learn to live with. Question 1, at the beginning of this book, encourages making a list of "must haves" and "can't stands" before entering a relationship, as a way of becoming conscious and clear about standards. If you find yourself in a relationship with someone who violates something on your list, are you selling your previous self down the river? Or have you evolved beyond what you previously thought was important?

"Accepting" means truly letting go of what was undesirable because you feel more than compensated and fulfilled by other factors. A key indicator of whether you have accepted something is that you don't think about it anymore. For example, you may have hoped for a partner who was tall, and then you find yourself with someone who is short. You may decide to continue the relationship with the short person because they bring many other things to the table that you value. After enjoying these benefits for a while, you find you hardly ever think about their height anymore because you are feeling fulfilled and loved overall.

"Settling" comes with a sense of deprivation and nagging disappointment. It often happens when a person feels forced to cope with a partner's shortcomings or bad behavior or is putting up with something undesirable out of fear (usually fear of rejection or losing the relationship or fear of conflict) rather than out of a sense that the undesirable thing is no longer important. "Settling" brings a sense of depressing resignation or loss of hope along with an increased propensity to fantasize about escape or relief. The human mind has a harder time "accepting" things that undermine integrity and wellness, which means that allowing ourselves to be neglected, mistreated, or dehumanized in some way is more likely to be a form of "settling." In other words, a partner who is rarely home and generally ignores you is harder to genuinely accept than a partner who is not as tall as you would have liked.

The lower a person's self-esteem, the more likely they are to feel a sense of desperation about being loved and validated and the more likely they are to settle for less than they deserve. They may tell themselves they are "accepting" their partner's shortcomings because at least that partner loves them, and that love brings a sense of validation or a sense of value that has never been felt before. If a person's only standard for a relationship is that they are loved, they are at much higher risk of settling for toxic experiences and situations.

39. What are the signs that my relationship may be in trouble?

Sometimes the most effective way to assess your relationship is to assess yourself. Consider questions such as:

- Am I healthy, both physically and mentally?
- Do I feel inspired, passionate, and free?
- Do I take responsibility for my own needs and growth?

- Do I respect the choices I make and make amends for my poor choices?
- Am I able to process resentment, anger, and fear productively?
- Do I respond to feelings of fear or insecurity with courage?
- Have I remained connected to my standards? Have I maintained friendships and hobbies apart from the relationship?
- Do I avoid trying to protect my ego and instead listen, even when what I'm hearing is unflattering?

If you answer no to any of those questions, you are hereby invited to set a goal of improving in that area. Taking that goal seriously will include assessing which of your current relationships support you moving in a healthy direction and which do not. The idea of your relationship being "in trouble" can be replaced with an honest assessment of what the relationship adds to or subtracts from your life and whether you can be the kind of person you want to be while maintaining that connection. If honest reflection and soul-searching uncovers uncomfortable truths about your relationship, then the relationship itself may be "in trouble," but you yourself may be very much on a path toward liberation and healing.

In 2008, Dr. Sue Johnson published her groundbreaking and influential guide to healing intimate partnerships, *Hold Me Tight*. At the core of her model is what she calls "demon dialogs," which, along with Gottman's "four horsemen of the apocalypse" (see question 14), can serve as signs that a relationship may need help to get on the right track. Johnson's three "demon dialogs" include:

1. *Find the bad guy:* A pattern of mutual blame and defensiveness that is born of a desire to protect the self (mainly the ego) by diverting attention to the other person's faults. Johnson describes how couples in this pattern go through stretches in which they lose touch with any emotion besides anger but may still reconnect intermittently.
2. *Protest polka:* One partner demands more connection and communication, and the other withdraws. Johnson describes both behaviors as a "protest" because they germinate from a perceived rejection or criticism by the other person. A person who is withdrawing may be engaged in a silent protest, a refusal to cooperate with what are seen as aggressive and critical tactics. This only triggers more demands from the other partner, who is desperately seeking rejoining and feeling like the silent partner doesn't care. (In the Gottman paradigm, this would be described as the criticism/stonewalling dynamic.)
3. *Freeze and flee:* Johnson describes this as the most troublesome pattern and the most difficult for a relationship to recover from. Couples

no longer fight. Instead there is "deadly silence." She explains, "This is what happens when the pursuing, critical partner gives up trying to get the [other's] attention and goes silent. If this cycle runs its course, the aggressive partner will grieve the relationship and then detach and leave." Mired in hopelessness, couples may revert to cordial communication and may even be able to function in superficial decision-making, but any sense of real intimacy is lost.

It does not take a trained couples therapist to see the agonizing dysfunction in the patterns described above. The greater question is what people are willing to do about them. Within all of those patterns are divisions of the self—acting in ways that we know are not productive, not loving, and not likely to improve the dynamic, and are therefore against our own interests. Continued failure to improve behavior and act more in concert with our values is a strong sign that the relationship will circle the drain unless help arrives from some sort of outside influence.

40. How do I find a good couples therapist?

As demand for mental health services continues to rise, finding any sort of counselor can be a challenge. The mistake many couples make is waiting until the relationship is on the brink of demise or waiting until a crisis moment to look for help. Depending on where you live and what your resources are, contacting therapists may result in being put on waiting lists while your relationship continues to struggle. A December 2021 *New York Times* article reported that about one-third of therapists surveyed in the United States had at least a three-month wait for an initial appointment.

One way to circumvent this problem is to form a relationship with a therapist before serious problems emerge. Looking for a therapist when you are not feeling highly stressed allows the freedom and clarity of mind to ask questions and be selective. Some therapists may be willing to schedule irregular or less-frequent appointments if your problems are not acute, and once you are on their caseload, you may have an easier time being seen more frequently should more serious problems emerge. Even if your relationship is in good shape, working on smaller problems or goals for improvement can help avert any bigger issues that might arise later on and can help you and your partner develop a comfort level with the therapist that could serve you well when and if the work becomes harder.

Below are some helpful questions to ask when shopping for a prospective therapist:

- How much experience do you have helping couples?
- Are you working with couples as your primary specialty?
- What books or resources do you most recommend for couples?
- What training or theories have most influenced your approach?
- Are you comfortable working with LGBTQ+ couples (if applicable)?
- Are you comfortable discussing or assisting in sexual matters? (A couples therapist who even hesitates in answering "yes" to this question would be best left off your list unless you are 100% certain there is nothing to work on regarding your sex life.)
- What is your approach when a person discloses something to you that they have not disclosed to their partner?
- How often do you find yourself aligning with one partner or the other? (An effective couples therapist will sometimes agree with one partner on specific issues or problems but will rarely align with one partner in a more general sense; in other words, they encourage both people to take responsibility as much as possible.)
- If you, yourself needed a couples therapist in this area, whom would you want to see?

Some clients like to ask if the therapist is happily married or in a long-term relationship. A certain answer (or the therapist's perceived comfort level in answering) may offer some peace of mind or a sense of relatability, but the relationship status of the therapist does not actually mean much in terms of outcomes. An oncologist does not need to have personally been stricken with cancer to more effectively help a person recover from cancer. Moreover, even if your counselor is not currently in a relationship, chances are they have some relationship experiences of their own to draw upon. A therapist who has been married for 25 years does not necessarily have a healthy marriage and does not necessarily have more to offer you than one who just got divorced for the second time. Sometimes there is more to be learned from failure than from success. Reputable therapists avoid discussing their own personal lives in much detail or depth so as not to make the conversation about themselves, so it's virtually impossible to tell how your therapist's own relationship status or history will influence their work.

At your first appointment, a good couples therapist will explain the format and expectations of the work before diving into the issues. If your therapist starts the appointment with a question like "So, what can I do for you?" they are probably not very experienced or skilled in couples work. Many individual therapists believe in a nondirective approach (the therapist's main job is supportive and empathic listening), but this tends to be less effective with couples because couples will simply repeat the same problematic dynamics that they are experiencing at home. While it may be helpful to some therapists to see these dynamics play out live, it can be harmful to invite this before there has been a complete explanation of what role this new third person in the room will be trying to play. Are they looking to mediate? Are they looking to arbitrate? Are they going to interrupt and coach better communication? Opening up the dynamics of your intimate partnership to a third person is a vulnerable thing to do, so it is wise to know what to expect from the therapist before you go down that road.

Endings

41. How do I know if it's time to move on from a relationship?

Ending a relationship, or setting new boundaries in a relationship, is a personal choice, based on your specific goals, values, and feelings. There are many layers of thinking and overthinking that lead up to this decision. For most people, the considerations differ depending on the length and circumstances of the relationship. A person you met a month ago has not earned as much loyalty as a person to whom you've been married for 20 years. "The grass is always greener on the other side of the fence" is an idiom you may find yourself pondering as you wonder if a different partner or life as a single person would really be preferable to the current relationship. Assessing whether or not your partner is "a good person" may further complicate the process; it is possible for two "good people" to be in a bad relationship.

Question 39 discusses things to consider in assessing how healthy or unhealthy your relationship may be. In deciding whether to move on from a relationship that is unhealthy or is not satisfactory to you, think about whether you believe the other person is willing and able to join with you to improve things that matter to you and whether you are willing to challenge yourself to grow and change for your partner, as well. For example, if you feel neglected by your partner because they are often preoccupied with other things, you may be looking for your partner to hear those concerns, take them seriously, and work toward change. Hopefully, you believe such a change would be good for your partner too, and not just for you. Are you similarly willing to hear and act on their concerns? If your partner wants to improve your sex life, for example, will you embrace the challenge and the opportunity for growth that may come with that, or are you simply not ready or willing to address that? Alternatively, can you and your partner come to genuinely accept limitations that can't or won't change? (See question 38 for more on "accepting" versus "settling.")

Couples who do not actively work on their relationship are doomed to watch it deteriorate, often to the point where conditions become intolerable and a breakup or divorce becomes the only obvious option. Simply put, if either you or your partner are not willing to listen and work together to make adjustments on each other's behalf, then it is worth examining why you would hold onto something that is only going to worsen. In many cases, a person feels little hope for the relationship but also feels afraid of the breakup, not wanting to inflict pain on a partner or perhaps feel regret. If the primary reason you have not ended a relationship is that you are afraid to hurt your partner's feelings, consider that you are hurting your partner in other ways by "leading them on" or by perpetuating something that is not truly what you want and deserve. Your partner may be hurt or even devastated by the breakup, but they will recover, and if they genuinely love you, then they will move through the grieving process and ultimately want you to find a relationship or a single life that feels truly nourishing to you.

42. How do I break up with a partner?

Often, a person searching for the best way or right way to do something is simply avoiding an unpleasant task. Once you decide that you want to end a relationship, the desire to find the right moment or method of doing so needs to be weighed against the ramifications of withholding that information. The sooner you tell the person you are breaking up, the sooner they can mourn the relationship and move on with their life. Ask yourself: Would my partner rather hear this news in the gentlest way possible and in the most convenient possible moment, even if it means letting them believe for a certain amount of time that you are still committed? What would you prefer if you were on the receiving end?

Breakups are painful. Here are some things to consider that may help mitigate any harm or pain for both parties:

1. It can be tempting to deflect responsibility for the decision to break up. Common methods for doing this include behaving badly (in hopes that the other person will initiate a break up), dropping hints, or trying to initiate conversation that you hope will result in a mutual decision to break up. Unfortunately, starting the conversation with something like "I've been feeling more distant from you" or "Sometimes I wonder if we are actually a good match" is more likely to confuse your partner, because it sounds like you want to address and work on something. If you actually want to build intimacy or explore more areas of common interest, then those statements are appropriate; if you actually mean to break up, then say so directly. A statement like "I need to end our relationship" or "I don't want us to be a couple anymore, but we can still be friends" would do the job.

2. Keep your self-respect. Communicate whatever you have to in a manner that allows you to feel you lived in accordance with your values. Should you break up over text or through a third party or in a face-to-face conversation? That depends on which decision you would respect more. If you feel the other person may react abusively or violently, then a text or phone breakup may be an appropriate way to protect yourself. Is it important to you to practice kindness? If so, then telling the other person that even though you feel the relationship has run its course, you value the role it has had in your life and that you wish them the best can help you stay in alignment with that value.

3. Allow the other person to have their emotions. You are under no obligation to try to soothe or fix the other person's pain. If you feel safe and empowered to do so, you may decide to answer their questions or discuss your feelings in more depth so they can understand what happened and come to a sense of finality, but if having that conversation does not feel right for you, the other person is capable of coming to terms with the breakup and handling their emotions with other resources. The other person may express anger toward you; you may decide to hear the other person's anger if it feels safe to do so, but you are not obligated to hear it and are certainly not obligated to change your mind in order to get the other person to stop being angry.

43. What do I do if my partner breaks up with me and I feel like my life is over?

Losing an intimate partner relationship can feel devastating. For some people, it can be hard to function normally for a time as the shock of this loss is absorbed. If you had envisioned building a future with the person, with marriage, family, or other dreams connected to them, then the task in front of you is to grieve not only the companionship and intimacy you had been experiencing, but the life you thought you were going to have. It is no small task. Still, it is crucial to remind yourself that you can grieve, heal, and recover to live a full and meaningful life and that the experience you gained in the relationship that just ended can help you enjoy healthier and more fulfilling relationships in the future.

In the immediate aftermath of a breakup, lean on the people you trust the most. Chances are there are family and friends who want to be there for you in some form or another. Most people experiencing the end of a significant intimate relationship need emotional support (a "shoulder to cry on," people who are safe to be vulnerable with) and logistical support (help with living arrangements or similar issues). You may have people in your life who are good at either or both. Others may be good for neither of those things but are available to simply spend time with so you don't have to be alone. There is nothing wrong with going to a friend's house and playing video games for a few hours just to feel a sense of normalcy and get a break from the hard work of picking up the pieces as long as you are not neglecting your other needs. Even if that friend offers you nothing else, you may still find yourself feeling grateful. Allow people to surprise you—sometimes meaningful support comes from people we didn't know cared that much.

Many people find counseling to be extremely helpful in recovering from a breakup, not only because it provides a designated space to acknowledge and process emotions, but also because it can help uncover insights about needs for personal growth and the role of that relationship in your life. Part of grieving is engaging a sense of gratitude to acknowledge the value the person had in your life, including the value of the hidden opportunities from the relationship ending when it did.

Sometimes a breakup is particularly crushing because a person's identity had been closely entwined in the partnership role. People will especially struggle to accept anything that feels like a threat to, or subtraction from, their identity or their sense of meaning and purpose in life. If you have a hard time seeing any reason to live outside of being in an intimate partnership, consider how much you might benefit from becoming more well rounded and embracing the other beautiful and meaningful experiences life has to offer. With time, you can come to view being single as an opportunity to become more balanced so that intimate partnership is one of many sources of gratification, rather than the only one (see question 31 on codependency).

44. Should my ex and I be friends?

In 2019, the *Atlantic*'s Ashley Fetters reported that the desire for people who used to date to maintain a friendship is a phenomenon that developed only in the last few decades, correlating with an increase in platonic friendships among all genders that is at least partially attributable to reduced clarity of, and adherence to, traditional community or gender roles. "The anxiety over 'I hope we can still be friends' likely stems from uncertainty over what exactly is meant by it, or whether the gesture is a sincere one," writes Fetters. "To utter it during a breakup conversation is either a kind and helpful way to lessen the pain of parting or the cruelest part of the whole endeavor, depending on who you ask. An attempt to stay friends may be a kindness if it suggests an attachment or a respect that transcends the circumstances of the romantic relationship, for instance. It can be a cruelty, however, when it serves to pressure the jilted party into burying feelings of anger and hurt."

Citing research by University of Kansas psychologist Rebecca Griffith, Fetters goes on to explain that people will seek to remain friends with an ex for one of four primary reasons:

1. Civility (the desire to inflict less pain by at least behaving cordially and politely).
2. Practicality (minimizing pain related to external circumstances, like shared workplace, children, or social circle).
3. Unresolved romantic feelings (the desire to remain connected to a person in case the option of dating them becomes appealing or available again).
4. Security (a high level of trust remains in the relationship despite an understanding that being romantic partners is no longer appropriate).

Griffith's research, published in 2017 in the journal *Personal Relationships*, found that ex-partners who remained friends for practicality or for security had more positive outcomes, while those who remained friends due to unresolved romantic feelings had negative outcomes. Unsurprisingly, ex-partner friendships that stemmed from a desire for civility or practicality were not sustained as well as those built on a sense of security.

Your feelings about whether or not to maintain a friendship with an ex-partner will likely depend on a few factors specific to the circumstances of your relationship and your life. If you have few other friends or low confidence in making friends, you may feel more of a desire to hold on to as much of the relationship as you can. If there was a breach of trust that led to the breakup, perhaps you feel that the area in which your ex is untrustworthy would not affect you in a friend role as much as it did in an intimate partnership. If you initiated the breakup, it can be tempting to offer friendship as a way of trying to take the sting out of the rejection for the other person (reassuring them that they are still valuable and important to you, just not in the role of romantic partner), but in those cases, you are only prolonging the inevitable pain of rejection unless your offer of friendship is authentic (if you were only trying to cushion the blow of rejection and didn't actually want to be friends, they will eventually figure it out as you struggle to keep motivated to engage in the "friendship").

Ultimately, if you feel your ex is a good person who is safe and worth knowing, even if they aren't "the one" for you, then it can be healthy to invite them to sustain a friendship. Hopefully, they feel the same way about you, even if they need some space first to process and grieve the end of the intimate partnership. As with many challenging relationship dynamics, clear and direct communication of boundaries and expectations can be helpful. Practice rigorous honesty with yourself and your ex about what level of contact feels appropriate and what you are both hoping to get out of the friendship. If either of you are wanting to be friends primarily to keep a pathway open to renew the romantic connection, consider taking some space from one another to allow time to grieve and move on before exploring a friendship.

45. My partner and I may need to live apart from each other. Is a long-distance relationship a good idea, or should we break up?

Long-distance relationships (often called LDRs) are surprisingly common, especially among young people. Studies suggest that between 25% and 50% of college students have LDRs at any one time, according to a 2013 article in *Science Daily*. The most common factors that drive geographic distance between lovers are the need to move for education or work, military service or deployment, and incarceration, not to mention relationships that begin as LDRs because the couple met online. Based on available research, the decision whether or not to maintain a relationship over geographic distance is best made by comparing the qualities of the relationship itself to one's overall life goals, rather than focusing too much on the issue of distance.

For example, consider the fictional couple Donna and Derek. They met in a biology class their first year of college and formed a quick bond through their senses of humor and mutual interests in music and movies. They have been a couple for about a year, but they don't quite have the same ideas about their future. Derek would like to get married and start a family right after graduation. Donna is more interested in exploring new places and experiences. In fact, she will be leaving in a couple of months to study abroad in Europe for a year. Derek has made it clear that he is willing to cope with an LDR for a year so they can be together after that, but he is not looking forward to the year apart. He expects to miss more regular intimacy and sense of availability and worries that Donna will be too busy to keep in touch with him. Donna feels excited about her opportunity and feels like occasional video calls will be enough to prevent her missing Derek significantly, as she will be absorbed in the new culture.

The above scenario illustrates a couple of potential problems that would make an LDR unsustainable. First, the short-term experiences are likely to be imbalanced. If both people feeling similarly about their own experience in each location (i.e., both excited or both dreading it but willing to cope), there is less fuel for resentment or jealousy (this dynamic is particularly prevalent in high school relationships where there is an age difference and the older person is planning to go away to college; for the older person, it is hard to avoid associating the relationship with a phase of life from which they are moving on). Second, the long-term goals for this couple are not quite compatible. Even if something interfered with Donna's study abroad plans and she was forced to stay home, the couple still has work to do to figure out how to merge their lifestyle goals after college. Notably, these same issues can pose challenges in geographically close relationships (GCRs) as well. Even a couple who lives together may find that one person is far more excited about their life outside the relationship than the other or that they may not have compatible visions for the future.

Perhaps that is why, contrary to conventional wisdom, LDRs are no less satisfying or successful than GCRs. A 2018 study published in the *Canadian Journal of Human Sexuality* found that even though people expect LDRs to be more challenging and less satisfying, those involved in them report levels of overall relationship satisfaction and sexual satisfaction similar to those in GCRs. This may have something to do with the mind valuing a sense of effort from a partner, and an LDR provides more opportunities to perceive our partner making a special effort. Couples in LDRs go above and beyond to compensate for the limits of needing to communicate electronically, according to Crystal Jiang and Jeffrey Hancock, authors of a 2013 study published in the *Journal of Communication*.

It can be helpful to remember that relationships take work to maintain, no matter the distance. Communicating directly, keeping things fresh and interesting by planning diverse activities, tending to trust and connection, and maintaining individual holistic wellness and integrity are all imperative for sustainable relationships, regardless of geography. Relationships should be enjoyed, not endured, says Kiaundra Jackson, a licensed marriage and family therapist interviewed by NPR in 2020. "You should be growing as an individual but also collectively," she says. "If you find yourself not doing that . . . you need to re-evaluate."

46. Is it healthy to date or hook up with someone new immediately after the end of a relationship?

It is common to experience the desire for what is often called "rebound sex," a "no strings attached" sexual encounter with someone new during the aftermath of a breakup. In a 2011 study published in the *Archives of Sexual Behavior*, almost 20% of those surveyed reported having sex with a new partner within four weeks of a breakup. Motivations for "rebound sex" may vary. The person who initiated the breakup may feel a sense of freedom and excitement from being able to partake in an activity (casual sex) that was, until recently, not okay (assuming the relationship was monogamous). The person who did not initiate the breakup may feel the urge to sleep with someone else out of spite or out of a desire to quell sadness for a while. Sometimes people want to boost their self-esteem and seek sexual experiences to reassure themselves that they can be desirable to potential new partners.

While there appears to be a potential sense of relief or excitement from a sexual encounter with a new person after a breakup, those benefits are temporary, and there is no evidence to suggest that such an encounter actually helps a person "get over" the breakup more quickly. Conversely, there is some research (a 2014 study published in the *Journal of Social and Personal Relationships*) that says those who enter a new dating relationship (beyond a one-time hookup) do feel better more quickly, harboring fewer negative feelings about the past relationship and feeling better about their own relational prospects and attractiveness. However, despite those benefits, the study authors found no difference in overall psychological well-being between those who entered "rebound relationships" and those who remained single. In other words, a rebound relationship may feel better, but it does not necessarily promote greater holistic mental wellness. Plus, there is some indication that the personal benefits of starting a new relationship quickly may be somewhat countered by the effects on the new relationship itself: namely, that you are more likely to compare your new partner to your old one or repeat mistakes made in the old relationship if you have not taken time to work on yourself. In other words, "rebound relationships" are not necessarily unhealthy, but they are also not typically sustainable.

The authors of the above study noted some limitations in their research—most significantly, that it was conducted only on college students, whose relationship histories tend, of course, to be shorter. The length and intensity of your recently ended relationship may influence your decision-making about whether to seek a new sex partner or dating opportunity right away. If you were in love for a significant amount of time, lived together, or were codependent (see question 31), it is likely wiser to budget more time for your own wellness before prioritizing a new connection. Likewise, if your desire for a new relationship stems from being unwilling to tolerate loneliness, consider that being "single" and being "lonely" are not the same thing. Connecting with friends, family, or community (i.e., clubs, churches, or recreational groups) can foster connections that serve as sustainable remedies for loneliness with or without the presence of a dating relationship in your life.

If you are considering a "hookup" or a new dating relationship immediately after a breakup, consider asking yourself these questions:

- Will I respect myself for this choice later?
- Am I feeling excited about the potential encounter/new relationship? Or am I just looking to numb or escape some pain? If it's the latter, how often am I willing to go to that well?
- Do I feel anxious about not being in a relationship? Is the new person truly impressing me, or am I just afraid to be single or lonely?
- Am I pursuing a hookup out of revenge, because I'm angry at my ex? If so, is that fair to my new sex partner? How will hurting my ex's feelings make my life better?
- Am I emotionally stable and mentally healthy enough to maintain safe sex practices or to set and maintain boundaries that will work for me?
- Did I experience or perpetrate abuse in my previous relationship? If so, how will I avoid repeating old patterns in my next relationship?

Also, see question 7 on hookups and question 17 on healthy sexual practices.

Case Studies

1. ARE MALCOLM AND LISA MORE THAN FRIENDS?

Malcolm and Lisa grew up playing together because their parents were friends in the same small town. They often attended the same birthday parties and almost always found themselves in the same classes through elementary and middle school. They both enjoyed music and theater; afternoons spent making up skits and songs together eventually emerged as participation in school performing arts programs. They each had leading roles in their high school musical during senior year. Aside from a month-long rift during the seventh grade after Malcolm refused Lisa's request for him to ask out one of her friends, they had always considered each other close friends.

Both Malcolm and Lisa had dreams of going to college out of state, but their families had limited resources, and both wound up at the same state university about two hours from their hometown. Feeling a bit overwhelmed at the size of the school and the city in which it was located, Malcolm sought out familiar faces to help ease anxiety during his first few months and often joined Lisa for BIO 100 study meetings that would more often than not turn into commiseration sessions. Before long, Malcolm noticed himself feeling emotionally and physically attracted to Lisa, which had never been the case before. Throughout middle and high school, friends would sometimes tease the two about their connection or suggest that they become a couple, but Malcolm was never particularly interested in dating, preferring to focus instead on schoolwork and video games. Serious attraction or romantic interest in someone was entirely new to him.

By Thanksgiving, Malcolm had decided that his feelings for Lisa were becoming too much of a preoccupation. He knew he needed to either share them with her or distance himself from her so that he could let the feelings die away and move on. After what felt like an eternity of anguished ambivalence, Malcolm sought the advice of a mutual friend, who told Malcolm that he should disclose his feelings to Lisa because even if she didn't share his feelings, their friendship was strong enough to withstand the awkwardness. He texted her that night.

For her part, Lisa considered Malcolm to be a friend only, almost like a brother; she did have a crush on him for a few months early in their high school years, but she assumed he wouldn't be interested and eventually moved on. By junior year, she had a serious boyfriend, but by the time senior prom rolled around, the relationship had gone stale. He headed to the military after graduation, and she felt a mixture of sadness and relief about the end of their relationship. Now that she was in college, she occasionally wondered if she and Malcolm would make a good couple someday, but for now, she was hoping to date more casually and see what it felt like to date and have sex with various guys. Though she had been enjoying hanging out and studying with Malcolm, receiving a text from him revealing the emergence of deeper feelings came as something of a shock. First, he asked if she had time to discuss something serious, and when she said yes, he wrote back, "I think I'm developing more serious, romantic-type feelings for you. I don't want to risk hurting our friendship, but I felt like it would be better to be open about this. If it's not something you're interested in, I will totally understand."

Lisa replied that she needed some time to think about it. After a couple of days, she wrote back, "Thank you for your honesty. I think you are the kind of guy who deserves a special relationship with someone devoted to you, and right now, I'm not interested in anything serious. Maybe someday the situation will change, but for now, I don't think it's a good idea." Though heartbroken, Malcolm respected the honesty and wisdom in Lisa's response. He said he would like to take a few weeks away from spending time together and focus on other interests. Malcolm visited the college counseling center for support dealing with his feelings. By February, they were hanging out together again in study sessions and at meals.

Analysis

Some of the most rewarding and long-lasting intimate partnerships are built on a foundation of friendship. In this case, such a development may still be on the cards for Malcolm and Lisa. As they continue to mature, their preferences and priorities about relationships will evolve, and they may eventually come to see each other as prime dating material.

In the meantime, reflecting on their feelings can yield some meaningful insights. Malcolm is showing signs that he may be demisexual, which means he experiences sexual or romantic interest only in the context of emotional intimacy. Though he and Lisa had been friends for most of their lives, in the context of adjusting to college, he had started to trust her more vulnerably and to feel closer to her as a result of sharing some feelings and experiences. Lisa may be more independent by nature, wanting to prioritize school and social interests over the work of maintaining a relationship, or she may be reacting against a recent relationship experience that she found stifling. Either way, she deserves the space to do what she feels is best for her.

Eventually, Malcolm decided he could trust Lisa with all of his true feelings, and thus, with the fate of their friendship. Though the rejection hurt, Malcolm will eventually see that his trust in Lisa was well founded—she made space for his feelings and held firm to her plan, demonstrating the type of integrity that Malcolm was coming to admire more and more. Malcolm respected Lisa's priorities for herself, choosing not to try to persuade her to reconsider. Even if they never become a couple, their friendship stands to flourish even more as a result of both of them taking advantage of the opportunity to respect and accept one another.

2. RAUL AND ALEX STRUGGLE WITH CODEPENDENCY AND ABUSE

Raul is a 19-year-old biology major who hopes to become a doctor. He grew up as a middle child in a family that emphasized the importance of education and pushed him hard to succeed in school. His parents worked hard to give their children a better life but were never particularly warm or attentive, especially toward Raul, who was always the most obedient and academically gifted of the three children and therefore did not require much pushing to succeed. "Raul is the one we never have to worry about," his mother would often say. Raul's siblings experimented with drugs, vandalism, shoplifting, and other rebellious behavior, but Raul always felt the need to follow the rules. He wanted his parents to accept, love, and feel proud of him, especially because he wasn't sure how they would feel if he ever decided to come out to them.

Though he struggled socially throughout his childhood, Raul did manage to make a couple of good friends soon after entering college. Near the start of his sophomore year, Raul met and fell in love with Alex, a charismatic and engaging 21-year-old who had overcome many hardships to make it to college. Alex was intensely curious and attentive toward Raul. The two of them would take long walks together at night, reveling in exciting and effortless discussions of their hopes for the future, their values, their favorite YouTube and TikTok influencers, and their backgrounds. Alex shared that he grew up in poverty and had been discouraged from going to college because of the expense. He told Raul about how his parents mainly viewed him as a burden and rarely took interest in him except to criticize him or blame him for things. After reaching adulthood, Alex arranged for his own mental health treatment and learned that he lives with PTSD and ADHD. His resentment toward his parents grew, as his academic path might have been easier if they had seen fit to find him care and advocate for accommodations.

The more Alex shared about the unfair treatment and neglect he had experienced in childhood, the more Raul admired him for his resilience, confidence, intelligence, and ambition. Whenever they disagreed, Alex seemed to be able to end the argument with a new fact or perspective that Raul had not considered before or did not know how to answer. Before long, Raul had Alex on a pedestal, deferring to Alex's judgment and preferences on a variety of topics. Meanwhile, Raul's friends noticed they were seeing less and less of him. Some saw signs of anger management problems and controlling behavior by Alex but did not know how to say anything to Raul without alienating him. After Raul and Alex moved in together, Raul became even less social. Much of his time was spent helping Alex stay organized, recover from panic attacks, or externally process the latest conflict with his parents. Raul missed his friends and some of the recreational activities he used to enjoy but felt it was more important for him to support Alex during times of need. Alex would become anxious or angry if Raul spent "too much" time away from home or connected meaningfully with other people. Alex's outbursts were particularly aggressive if he had been drinking, which did not happen all the time, but happened often enough to be impactful. He would try to make Raul feel guilty by pointing out things he had done for him in the past. If Alex had been drinking and felt alarmed that

Raul was disengaging, he would sometimes panic and cut himself, which frightened Raul and prompted him to tend even more to Alex out of fear for his safety.

Meanwhile, Raul was starting to feel more confident and validated in other areas of his life, such as academics (where he excelled) and his part-time job at a local restaurant, where he was lauded for his work ethic and leadership skills, offered a promotion, and frequently invited to social outings with other employees. These experiences contrasted with his experiences in the relationship, where things seemed to be getting worse despite his desperation to rekindle a positive connection. With anxiety boiling over and Alex refusing to try couples therapy or substance abuse counseling due to negative experiences with therapists in the past, Raul sought counseling for himself, where he was able to gain more clarity about his own values and identity and eventually realized he was feeling overburdened in his relationship. He approached Alex and angrily demanded changes, mainly that Alex go to therapy to deal with his trauma and find other resources to help him stay organized and manage anger. Alex felt betrayed and became defensive. He insisted that Raul was exaggerating or making up the problems and resented the implication that he was a burden because of his past. Raul began to doubt his own sanity, thinking that maybe Alex was right and he was construing everything in a faulty way. With the discussion having dissolved into a stubborn, silent stalemate interrupted by occasional bickering, Raul found himself obsessing over nonsensical escape fantasies and sexual urges. He panicked about the possibility that he was crazy and checked himself into a local psychiatric hospital. His experiences there helped him realize he could not remain mentally healthy in a relationship with Alex, and he broke up with Alex after being released from the hospital.

Analysis

Abuse that does not come in the form of physical violence or outright bullying can still have devastating psychological consequences, particularly because the "less severe" forms of abuse can be harder to notice if you have not learned to pay attention to them. In this example, Raul experiences gaslighting (the denial of another person's reality) and guilt-tripping (a form of manipulation), which are forms of psychological abuse. Raul entered the relationship vulnerable to these kinds of tactics because his own lack of confidence in himself, and his residual desires to please an authority figure prompted him to hand over power to Alex that Alex may not have consciously wanted. Alex most likely sensed Raul's passivity and neediness and tried to make Raul happy by supplying what seemed to be missing (expertise and decisiveness), inadvertently eroding Raul's confidence in the process and perpetuating a power imbalance.

It is notable that things shifted in the relationship as Raul gained confidence through other experiences. This upended the dynamic; suddenly, Alex did not have as much control as he was used to. Conflict increased, as Raul no longer felt as comfortable subverting his own preferences to avoid Alex feeling upset. Paradoxically, as Raul felt better about himself, he was feeling worse overall, because his sense of wellness continued to be almost entirely tied into his sense of whether he was in good standing with Alex. Having time away from Alex during his hospitalization and having the chance to open up to supportive professionals about what he had been experiencing, enabled Raul to gain clarity about the toxicity in their dynamic and how much it was affecting him.

As was mentioned in questions 29 and 31, countless relationships are affected by mental illness or substance abuse, but that does not mean they are all codependent relationships. People who live with any sort of disorder do everyone in their life a favor when they take ownership of it rather than denying it. They develop a network of resources to help heal the disorder or at least keep it at bay. In this example, both Raul and Alex have much to learn about what resources they need to become healthier. Raul has the opportunity to become more independent, building his integrity, and a more complete sense of identity that will enable him to bring more to the table in his future relationships. Alex has the opportunity to take stock of his own poor coping methods, including substance abuse and pressuring others to help him at their own expense, and embrace the hard work of genuinely healing from the past.

3. JAKE TELLS CHARLOTTE HE WANTS AN OPEN RELATIONSHIP

Charlotte and Jake knew each other throughout high school because they both played varsity basketball and had several mutual friends. They dated other people off and on and never really noticed each other until hooking up at a party one night toward the end of their senior year. After that, they continued to see each other for a few weeks, mostly for sex, until Charlotte discovered she was pregnant. She briefly considered terminating the pregnancy but decided against it and told Jake that he was going to be a father. Jake vowed to support Charlotte and the baby as well as he could. His own father had never participated much in his life, and Jake was determined not to repeat that choice.

After graduation, Jake got a job painting houses for his uncle's business. Determined to make the best future possible for his child, he worked 60–70 hours a week, while Charlotte attended classes at a local community college, working on an associate degree in respiratory therapy. They considered themselves a couple but actually saw very little of each other, especially after their son was born, and they found themselves tag-teaming childcare responsibilities while still juggling work and school. Though they would enjoy one another's company during rare meals or evenings together, there was little romance. They did make it a point to have sex about once a week, but it had grown somewhat stale and perfunctory and neither felt comfortable enough talking about sex to advocate for anything different.

Charlotte had a number of health problems during and after the pregnancy, and even with some help from her family, Jake still felt overwhelmed trying to work and take care of his partner and the house. He slept only about four hours per night. In rare down moments, he would get lost in his phone. He felt trapped and depressed, with no relief or solutions in sight. He spent more and more time looking at pornography and even found himself making an online dating profile, even though he promised himself he would never actually meet up with anyone.

One day, Jake overheard Jeff, one of his new coworkers, talking about his "open relationship" with his girlfriend, in which they both agreed they could have sexual encounters with other people as long as there were no romantic feelings or attachments involved. Jake had heard of this kind of arrangement before but always assumed they never worked out. Jeff said he and his girlfriend had been together for years and had never been happier. He had always felt guilty noticing other women, either in the media or when he was out in public, but now he was starting to think of how freeing it would feel to be able to explore new connections. He arrived home from work that night and announced to Charlotte that he now identified as nonmonogamous and would be dating other people. Charlotte was crushed. She felt betrayed on multiple levels. She was incensed that Jake would take up any new hobby that would pull his attention away from the needs at home, never mind a hobby that she felt would threaten their already fragile romantic connection. She wanted to know why she was not enough for him and why he would risk being pulled away from his family after all the promises he made. Jake countered that Charlotte was stifling his innate sexuality and should support him being more authentically himself. He insisted he was still committed to being the best partner and father he could be, and he believed being more free sexually would pull him out of his depression.

Unable to get through to one another, the relationship reached a stale-mate. After a few weeks, Charlotte confided in her sister that she and Jake were struggling, and her sister asked their other siblings to pitch in with childcare and money to help pay for couples therapy.

Analysis

There are valid feelings on both sides of this quandary but also a few mis-takes. Jake is right to feel there is no shame in being attracted to other people—it is very common for people in healthy, committed relationships to experience attraction to, or temporary infatuation with, people outside the relationship. He is also right that this could be considered an innate part of his sexuality. However, he is confused about "identifying" as non-monogamous. Nonmonogamy is a practice, not an identity. Some people identify as polyamorous, meaning they can be in love with, or romantically involved with, more than one person at the same time. Sexual attraction is not the same as love. Last, it is healthy for Jake to be transparent about his sexuality, but announcing a new arrangement is not a very cooperative way to address a problem that affects both him and his partner. A more respectful approach would be to name his feelings and desires and ask for a cooperative discussion about how to proceed. It is possible that Jake is unwittingly trying to use sexual outlets to self-medicate his depression. It may be wise for him to address the depression itself and explore its other possible causes (such as feeling trapped in a relationship and unable to pursue the future he might have imagined for himself before becoming a father or chemical/genetic reasons or unhealed childhood wounds). Once his depression improves, he can then notice if his urges to seek sex outside the relationship remain the same.

Charlotte's jealousy is understandable, as is her anger about the under-standing between them being changed without her consent. She would be within her rights to insist that Jake do more to work on their own struggling relationship rather than exploring others. Nonmonogamous arrangements generally work only when everyone involved is consenting to the arrangement, when there is transparency, and when the relation-ships are healthy and mutually satisfying. Jeff was describing a relationship that was already thriving, with or without outside partners. Introducing a practice of nonmonogamy to a relationship that is on the rocks is not likely to improve matters.

Charlotte's belief that Jake's desire to explore other sexual connections means that she is "not enough for him" is likely erroneous. Many people feel attracted to and satisfied by their partner but still have an appetite for other connections. In these cases, it's not a matter of being "enough" sexually any more than a partner's choice to go out to eat once in a while means that the cooking served at home is "not enough." Still, her insecurities are valid and deserve a place in the conversation. Not everyone is ready for a nonmonogamous relationship, and no one should have one forced upon them.

4. CONFLICT ARISES WHEN SAM AND YUNG-WEI MOVE IN TOGETHER

Sam and Yung-Wei felt they had a storybook romance, until they moved in together. They had met at an orientation event before their first year of college. They were paired off during an icebreaker, and Yung-Wei immediately felt attracted to Sam's bubbly and energetic personality, while Sam was drawn to Yung-Wei's maturity and intelligence. There was instant chemistry, followed by frequent texting, followed by long walks together around campus late at night. Though both had thought they would stay single and not commit too strongly to one person, by mid-October, they could not deny they were in love.

Both Sam and Yung-Wei thrived throughout freshman year as individuals and as a couple. They were mindful to take space and pursue their own interests, friendships, and opportunities outside the relationship. Arguments were rare and quickly discarded with heartfelt apologies. They found it relatively easy to respect and support one another and felt they were on the same page about nurturing their connection throughout college so they could marry and have children after graduation.

By springtime, Yung-Wei had decided he did not want to live on campus anymore, primarily because of late-night noisiness in the residence hall. He and Sam discussed the idea of finding an apartment together. It felt like the next natural step in their relationship and made financial sense for both of them. They signed a one-year lease in June.

Unfortunately, within a few weeks, they were already struggling. Arguments occurred almost every day, usually about household chores and cleanliness. Yung-Wei was managing his obsessive-compulsive disorder with medication and therapy but still much preferred a tidy and sanitized living environment. Sam, who identifies as nonbinary, wanted to respect their partner's sensitivities, but their ADHD made it particularly challenging to change certain habits, such as dropping things on the floor upon returning home, leaving food items out on the counter, or not wiping down the bathroom sink after brushing their teeth. In their family of origin, Sam's mother always took care of the cleaning, including picking up after other people's messes. Sam agreed that their habits were thoughtless and inconsiderate, but they also resented Yung-Wei's critical and sometimes contemptuous tone when he would vent his frustration about their failure to adjust to his needs. Yung-Wei had grown up with authoritarian parents and a hierarchical power structure, and as one of the oldest siblings, he was used to ordering others around and getting his way. Sam also comes from a family in which conflicts were swept under the rug rather than addressed and resolved, so they feel a lot of anxiety when Yung-Wei tries to hold them accountable for things.

With these new challenges, it became clear to both of them that the hasty apologies were no longer cutting it. One night they sat down after dinner to figure out what to do. They both agreed that their bond was important, but even if they were not going to remain a couple, they were stuck in a lease together and had to figure out how to get along. Sam agreed to browse for books and podcasts about settling domestic differences, and Yung-Wei promised to sign them up for couples counseling at their college's counseling center. Having committed to work together and take actions, they each left the conversation feeling more trusting and hopeful.

Analysis

Differing cultures and clashing mental health symptoms pose sudden, unanticipated challenges for this hopeful couple. When not trying to coexist in the same living space, two people can avoid triggering one another pretty easily. In the home environment, people tend to replicate the way of being they learned in the household in which they grew up, which can exacerbate cultural differences. The way a person might mute their anxieties or reactions in public goes out the window in the home, where most folks expect to be able to be more authentically themselves. With Sam and Yung-Wei's relationship facing its first real test, they are responding with loyalty and teamwork, despite ongoing frustrations.

Transformative conflict resolution, in which the two sides essentially work to understand and empathize with one another better, offers little utility in this scenario, because this couple already understands each other pretty well. They have taken the time to learn about the challenges and limitations of each other's illnesses. They have listened respectfully to each other's cultural experiences and have gone out of their way to learn about each other's cultural background from outside sources. They feel compassion for each other and a desire to return to connection, but they find that their own anxieties still get in the way in heated moments. They need to develop the negotiating skills that will allow them to respect one another's autonomy without simply grabbing for more power.

Just as Sam needs to learn to work with conflict rather than avoiding it and to be more considerate by taking responsibility for cleaning up their messes, Yung-Wei needs to adjust to a system of sharing power rather than expecting compliance. With help, the two of them can brainstorm compromises or creative solutions. Each must be willing to give up some of what they want so they can arrive at a solution they can mutually live with. For example, they may decide that Yung-Wei will take over cleaning responsibilities, including picking up after Sam, in exchange for Sam being responsible for cooking meals and doing laundry. They may also decide that there are certain types of messes that Yung-Wei must challenge himself to tolerate, at least for a while (this goal would probably fit in well with his OCD treatment), in exchange for Sam being willing to do 15 minutes of tidying before they go to bed each night. None of these solutions will fix the entire problem, but they will represent a step forward in developing a culture of teamwork and trust as they continue to learn and adapt to one another's needs.

5. ASHLEIGH GRAPPLES WITH BOUNDARIES, SELF-RESPECT, AND POWER DYNAMICS

Ashleigh had struggled throughout childhood to make friends and feel accepted. She was mostly ignored in school and occasionally bullied for being overweight, but by age 15, puberty had brought a growth spurt that evened out her figure, and she was noticing the change in how others reacted to her, particularly boys. At first, she recoiled from the attention and retreated further into the comforts of books and academic work. Then a teacher convinced her to join the debate team, where she met a charismatic older girl named Leah who decided to take Ashleigh under her wing. Leah had a big heart and often loved to help those who looked like they needed a friend.

After a few weeks of social media chatting and having lunch with Leah and her friends, Ashleigh was starting to think of herself as part of a social group for the first time in her life. She felt excited and hopeful, but also anxious, as her mind was filled with worries about how she might say or do something wrong and become exiled. As she became closer to Leah, she mentioned how much she envied Leah's comfort with socializing and wanted to learn to make friends more easily. When Leah invited Ashleigh to come along to a party being thrown by some members of the football team, Ashleigh felt like she had to accept the invitation or risk losing her new social standing. Having only experienced high school parties from the media, she did not feel ready. She assumed she would be expected to drink or have sex with someone she barely knew. She confided her concerns to Leah, who promised to look out for her. Leah told Ashleigh that she was proud of her for trying something new and that the experience would be good for her social life.

As it turned out, Ashleigh was just fine at the party. She enjoyed the music and laughed at some of the antics but felt mostly bored. Then she found herself talking with a 19-year-old named Nathan who had graduated the year before but was still friends with some of the football players. Nathan was handsome and funny, and Ashleigh felt surprised to be talking with him. He asked her about her favorite books and seemed genuinely interested. They had just added each other on social media when Leah interrupted the conversation to report that she needed to scoot home, and since she was Ashleigh's ride, it meant the night was over for her too.

Ashleigh woke up the next morning feeling a huge sense of relief from the loneliness she had experienced in most of her life to that point, but also some continuing anxiety about how she might still inadvertently torpedo all this progress. Eyes still groggy, she reached for her phone to see the time and was surprised to see a message from Nathan, thanking her for a fun conversation and wondering about her plans for the rest of the weekend. Ashleigh had family obligations but wound up messaging back and forth with Nathan all day, sharing memes, selfies, and updates on each other's day.

This was the beginning of about four days of steady contact between the two. Ashleigh felt excited to be getting all this attention for multiple reasons. Nathan was attending college about four hours away, but he was still well known and well connected at her school, and if word of their connection spread, it would only help her social standing. Plus, experiencing interest from a charming and handsome boy felt like a dream come true compared to her life just a few months prior.

The next Friday night, about five days after the party where they had met, things became sexual between Ashleigh and Nathan over messaging. Nathan asked what she was wearing and then talked about wanting to hold her and kiss her passionately. Ashleigh froze up reading these words, and the only thing she could think to do was reciprocate them. Nathan then shared a selfie with his shirt off and asked her to do the same. Ashleigh felt a jolt of panic but then rationalized that with a bra on, it wasn't much different than a bathing suit photo. Nathan replied with some more sexual talk, and Ashleigh was feeling her hormones flowing. Then he asked for a topless photo. At first, Ashleigh declined, but Nathan said it would help him feel closer to her and that he wanted to feel closer to her, as the miles between them were difficult and he didn't know if he could continue his interest in her if she wasn't willing to express her feelings for him more deeply. Reluctantly, Ashleigh sent the requested photo and begged Nathan not to share it with anyone.

Ashleigh struggled to fall asleep that night, feeling uneasy with herself about what she had done. At school Monday morning, she noticed some of the football players laughing and pointing at her from across the cafeteria, and she knew she had made a huge mistake.

Analysis

This story illustrates some of the hazards of relationships between people of unequal power or vulnerability. The age difference between Nathan and Ashleigh is an obvious red flag. While four years is not much of an experience gap for middle-aged people, it can be a giant chasm for those in their teens. The person with less experience is also often the person with lower confidence and is more likely to defer to the other person for guidance, particularly if that person is charismatic. Ashleigh's anxiety about losing social standing represents a hypervigilant response to the trauma of past bullying, which makes her vulnerable to those who could take advantage of her eagerness to be accepted. The corrupting influence of power is well documented throughout human history, and the truth of that aphorism manifests just as much in interpersonal relationships as in politics or business. A person with otherwise honorable or kind intentions may unwittingly succumb to acts of manipulation and abuse that often start out as more subtle but no less dangerous than the blatant act of betrayal described here.

Even partners who are the same age may experience imbalances of power or vulnerability. Sometimes problems arise not from concrete or measurable forms of power, such as physical strength and money, but from the amount of vulnerability felt by one person compared to the other. In this vignette, Ashleigh felt her sense of psychological safety was riding on Nathan's approval. This is not unlike the controversy that emerged in 2017 surrounding comedian Louis C. K. after several women accused him of sexual misconduct, all alleging that he had coerced them into watching him masturbate. The comedian at first denied the allegations and then defended himself by saying he had obtained verbal consent. His explanation failed to account for the fact that the women involved believed he had power over their careers and therefore felt pressure to avoid incurring his disappointment or anger. A person holding more power has a responsibility to empathize with those who hold less. In the above story, Nathan fails to reflect on what the relationship might be like for Ashleigh. He may believe nude images are no big deal and she should not take things so seriously, but this belief is enabled by a reckless lack of consideration of another person's reality, let alone her expressed wishes. It would not have taken much for him to notice her lack of confidence and experience and to accept some responsibility for empowering her rather than blindly seeking what he wanted. Unfortunately, people who are in denial of their own power are often just as dangerous as those who actively seek to wield power over those in weaker positions.

Leah serves as a contradicting example of how to handle a power imbalance in a healthy way. With greater social capital and greater experience, Leah decides to empower her new friend by serving as a guide and protector. It is likely that she tried to save Ashleigh from greater danger on the night of the party by interrupting her conversation with Nathan. She knows that Ashleigh lacks confidence and retreats to her comfort zone (books) too often. Crucially, Leah does not take control and try to "fix" Ashleigh against her will. She joins with Ashleigh's own goal of improving her social life and encourages her in taking the needed steps. Ashleigh was wise to stretch herself by embracing some new experiences with the help of a trustworthy ally.

Ashleigh's story also demonstrates the importance of thinking through boundaries before a relationship happens. If anyone had asked her a month prior to these events if she would ever share nude photos of herself with an adult, she would have thought it was a ridiculous idea. Although people will sometimes change their minds, there is a much greater chance of adhering to boundaries if you have thought through what your boundaries are in advance.

Glossary

Abuse: Any act that dehumanizes another living being by means of physical or psychological harm.

Accepting: As contrasted with "settling" (see below), the act of letting go of resistance to past or present conditions to make room for empowered choices and goal-setting.

Aggressiveness: Prioritizing one's own rights, needs, or preferences above another person's.

Assertiveness: Communicating one's own rights, needs, or preferences directly and with equal regard for the rights, needs, or preferences of others.

Attachment Styles: Patterns of relating or bonding with other people, generally categorized as anxious (or preoccupied), avoidant (or dismissive), disorganized (or anxious-avoidant), or secure. Attachment styles are determined primarily by caregiver attention patterns experienced in early childhood.

Boundaries: Direct personal experiences that a person has told others they are unwilling to have.

Codependence: The attempt to establish an identity or a sense of safety through a role or relationship or a preoccupation with helping a needy person or people with the unintended consequence of neglecting one's own needs.

Consent: Explicitly communicated agreement to participate in an activity or experience.

Contempt: As defined by Gottman, an attitude of critical superiority to another person or other people, generally communicated as disgust, hostility, or cruelty.

Criticism: As described by Gottman, generalized attacks on a person's personality traits or behavior patterns.

Defensiveness: As described by Gottman, the act of arguing against perceived criticism as a means of attempting to preserve a sense of good standing and stable bond.

Empowerment: The act of encouraging, enabling, or supporting a person in the attempt of meeting their own goals.

Forgiveness: The act of releasing anger (may or may not lead to renewal of relationship or rebuilding of trust).

"Friends with Benefits" Arrangement: An arrangement in which two or more consenting individuals agree to a sexual relationship without romantic commitment or attachment.

Hookup Culture: Group norms or values in particular locations or social structures tending to emphasize a normalizing of, or preference for, sexual encounters without relationship commitment or expectation of monogamy.

Intimacy: The sharing of personal and potentially vulnerable information or experiences with another person.

Intimate Partner Violence: An act that threatens or compromises the physical or psychological safety of an intimate partner.

Jealousy: The fear of losing a bond or being replaced as a priority to another person.

Love Language: A term coined by Dr. Gary Chapman to describe the five different preferences or tendencies by which people express and receive feelings of affection.

Monogamy: The practice of maintaining a sexual relationship with one partner.

Passivity: As contrasted with "aggressiveness" (see above), prioritizing others' rights, needs, or preferences above one's own.

Polyamory: The practice or identification of feeling romantic love with more than one person at a time and maintaining multiple intimate or romantic relationships at the same time.

Privacy: As contrasted with "secrecy" (see below), the practice of withholding information from a person who may not be trusted to handle the information responsibly or who does not have a right to the information.

Secrecy: As contrasted with "privacy" (see above), the practice of withholding information from a person or people even though they could be trusted to handle the information responsibly or they have a right to know the information.

Settling: As contrasted with "accepting" (see above), the act of resigning oneself to a nonpreferred future in a way that compromises integrity and fails to advocate for compromises or improvements.

Sexual Assault: A sexual act that takes place without the explicit consent of everyone involved, including when a person lacks the capacity to consent due to age or due to the influence of alcohol or other drugs.

Standards: Expectations or quality benchmarks that a person adopts for a specific purpose (in this context, for traits they are seeking in a relationship or a romantic partner).

Stonewalling: As defined by Gottman, the act of disengaging from a conflict with silence of physical distance for a sustained and indefinite period of time.

Transactional Conflict Resolution: A strategy for resolving conflict that focuses on negotiation and compromise rather than trying to change the other party's feelings, priorities, motivations, or perspective.

Transformative Conflict Resolution: A strategy for resolving conflict that focuses on increasing understanding and empathy between parties, thus potentially healing and restoring trust and opening pathways for problem-solving.

Directory of Resources

BOOKS

Beattie, Melody. *Codependent No More*. Center City, MN: Hazelden, 1986. ISBN: 9780894864025
This book offers a standard-bearing explanation of codependency and guide to developing a healthier identity.

Dana, Deb. *The Polyvagal Theory in Therapy*. New York: W.W. Norton & Company, 2018. ISBN: 9780393712377
This book elucidates how the brain subtly reads cues from those around us (especially those with whom we are intimate) for safety and stability and what can be done to facilitate grounding and calm in relationships.

Hendrix, Harville, and Helen LaKelly Hunt. *Getting the Love You Want*. New York: St. Martin's Press, 2019. ISBN: 9781250310538
This book offers an introduction to imago therapy, which focuses on ways to work with the influence of early childhood experiences on adult relationships to facilitate intimacy.

Johnson, Sue. *Hold Me Tight*. New York: Little, Brown and Company, 2008. ISBN: 9780316113007
This book introduces emotionally focused therapy for couples and self-help resources for positive conversations to disrupt negative patterns.

Lancer, Darlene. *Codependency for Dummies*. Hoboken, NJ: Wiley, 2015. ISBN: 9781118982082
This book provides a useful introduction to codependency and guide for self-assessment.

Rosenberg, Marshall. *Nonviolent Communication*. Encinitas, CA: Puddle-Dancer Press, 2015. ISBN: 9781892005281
This book explains the principles and practices of learning to listen powerfully and respectfully and to articulate directly and responsibly.

Tutu, Desmond, and Andrea Mpho. *The Book of Forgiving*. New York: HarperCollins, 2015. ISBN: 9780062203571
This book lays out four steps to letting go of anger and old wounds so that healing can take hold.

CHANNELS AND PODCASTS

Steph Anya, LMFT

www.youtube.com/c/StephAnya
This popular YouTube channel breaks down important concepts and offers helpful tips on a variety of topics connected to relationships and family dynamics.

Attachment Theory in Action

www.attachmenttheoryinaction.podbean.com
This podcast features nationally recognized experts and researchers on attachment and trauma.

Jon Gordon

www.youtube.com/user/JonGordonSelects
The ideas Jon Gordon presents in his books and on his YouTube channel focus on success in business and team scenarios but are often easily applicable to intimate relationships.

Neurodiverse Love

https://www.neurodiverselove.com/podcast-3
This podcast and website is devoted to empowering those on the autism spectrum to improve their relationships.

Where Should We Begin

www.estherperel.com/podcast

Influential couples therapist Esther Perel focuses on real-life case studies mixed with the unique, provocative, and highly influential host offering analysis along the way.

Your Diagnonsense

www.toddsbaratz.com/podcast-yd

This podcast, hosted by licensed relationship counselor and sex therapist Todd Baratz, explores a wide range of issues related to sexuality.

HOTLINES

All-Options

1-888-493-0092

www.all-options.org

This resource offers unbiased help with decision-making about pregnancy.

National Domestic Violence Hotline

1-800-799-7233

www.thehotline.org

A safe number to call if you are experiencing intimate partner violence or have concerns.

National Sexual Assault Hotline

1-800-656-4673

www.rainn.org

RAINN (Rape, Abuse, and Incest National Network) is the largest organization fighting sexual violence in the United States.

WEBSITES

ADHD and Marriage

www.adhdmarriage.com

Dr. Melissa Orlov, a leading expert on the impact of ADHD on relationships, has packed her site with blog entries, community forums, seminars, and links to other information and resources.

Advocates for Youth

www.advocatesforyouth.org

This Washington, DC, based organization works to help young people make healthy choices about sex and sexuality.

Co-Dependents Anonymous

www.coda.org

Here you can find literature and facts about codependency as well as search tools to find meetings.

The Gottman Institute

www.gottman.com

This site contains valuable articles, videos, and other resources and programs for couples.

Harriet Lerner

www.harrietlerner.com

This influential psychologist offers numerous books and blog entries on the topic of anger and accountability.

The National Coalition Against Domestic Violence

www.ncadv.org

This site offers a wealth of facts and self-directed coursework along with some guidance on how to take action on the issue politically.

Planned Parenthood

www.plannedparenthood.org

Both this site and the Planned Parenthood YouTube channel are good sources of information about pregnancy and sexual health.

The Trevor Project

www.thetrevorproject.org

This organization supports and connects LGBTQ+ youth.

The U.S. Centers for Disease Control and Prevention—Sexual Health

www.cdc.gov/sexualhealth

This government resource provides authoritative and current data and medical facts about sexually transmitted infections, pregnancy, and so on.

Index

About the Author

Charles A. McKay, LCPC, practices psychotherapy in Brewer, Maine. He specializes in relationships, trauma recovery, and depression. In his spare time, he enjoys kayaking, board games, and improv comedy.